Thousands of Pieces of Silver and Gold

Thousands of Pieces of Silver and Gold

Tracing the golden thread of grace through every Psalm

By
Janice Stauffer MacLeod

XULON PRESS

Xulon Press
2301 Lucien Way #415
Maitland, FL 32751
407.339.4217
www.xulonpress.com

© 2020 by Janice Stauffer MacLeod

All rights reserved solely by the author. The author guarantees all contents are original and do not infringe upon the legal rights of any other person or work. No part of this book may be reproduced in any form without the permission of the author. The views expressed in this book are not necessarily those of the publisher.

Unless otherwise indicated, Scripture quotations taken from the Holy Bible, New International Version (NIV). Copyright © 1973, 1978, 1984, 2011 by Biblica, Inc.™. Used by permission. All rights reserved.

Scripture quotations taken from the King James Version (KJV) – *public domain.*

Printed in the United States of America.

ISBN-13: 978-1-6305-0394-9

Dedicated

To my parents who gave me a childhood overflowing with books and who taught me from an early age to treasure God's Word.

The law from Your mouth is more precious to me than thousands of pieces of silver and gold.

(Psalm 119:72)

Introduction

No book of the Bible-for that matter, no book ever-tugs at the heartstrings the way and to the extent that the book of Psalms does. Located in the center of the Bible, it is a song book, a prayer book, a book of confessions, praises, and pleading all wrapped into one. God-breathed, the words were scribed by at least seven human authors and organized into five sections, each corresponding to a book in the Pentateuch (the books of the Law).

I. **Genesis Section:** Psalms 1-41; written mainly by David when experiencing some of the most troubling times of his life, his heartfelt pleas alternating with praise lead the reader to realize God's persistent protection and His ever-present help for all who earnestly cry out to Him.

II. **Exodus Section:** Psalms 42-72; this section focuses on God as the almighty King, just Judge, and the righteous rescuer of His own from His enemies. He is the ruler yet!

III. **Leviticus Section:** Psalms 73-89; this section showcases God's presence and His faithfulness to His people through the generations, even until now.
IV. **Numbers Section:** Psalms 90-106; inspiring the reader to look up, this section helps us focus our eyes on the unseen yet majestic Lord and to respond with unbridled praise and adoration.
V. **Deuteronomy Section:** Psalms 107-150; the final section overflows with thanksgiving and praise for a God who saves, delivers, and dwells among us. Here we uncover the vast storehouse of treasures God has in His Word for those who seek truth.

Meet the writers of the Psalms:

David: The poet, shepherd, and king authored half of the Psalms or more over the course of his lifetime. The dramatic story of how the shepherd boy became the second king of Israel is told in detail in 1 Samuel 1-2 and 1 Chronicles 1-2. These books are good companion reading to the many Psalms that are credited to David. Scribed while both soaring with joy and drowning in despair, David's prayers are open, honest, and candid. They teach us how to pray honestly and openly.

Asaph and sons: This family, which authored twelve of the Psalms, were ordained as worship leaders by King David. The central Psalm, 119, dedicated to the love of God's Word, is the theme of this book and is credited to Asaph.

The sons of Korah: This family was part of the tribe of Levi, the priestly division of the Israelites. In response to Korah's rebellion against Moses and Aaron (Numbers 16), God caused the earth to swallow him. Graciously, God permitted his sons to continue to serve in the house of the Lord and ultimately to write eleven beautiful Psalms that inspire us yet today.

Solomon: The son of David, when ordained as King of Israel, asked his father to pray that he might have wisdom (1 Kings 3). Best known as the writer of other books of wisdom-Proverbs, Ecclesiastes, and Song of Solomon-Solomon also authored Psalms 72 and 127.

Moses: The leader of the Israelites in their exodus out of Egypt and their journey to the Promised Land, Moses authored the five books of the Law recording the amazing story. He also authored the ninetieth Psalm, one of the most beautiful and poignant of the Psalms.

Ethan the Ezrahite and Heman: Each authored one Psalm (88, 89). Though little is known about either of these men, we know they were considered wise, as noted in 1 Kings 4:31.

Why Psalms? Why now?

Discouraged by the depressing news cycles; the confusing chaotic thinking I was exposed to daily through casual conversations with colleagues and acquaintances; the divisiveness so apparent in the country; and the escalation, acceptance, and celebration of lies and deluded thinking in our society, I turned to the Psalms, giving myself the luxury of spending as long as I needed on each one until the message was fully instilled in me. What follows are the lessons learned, Psalm upon Psalm as I journeyed through the Psalms, letting their life-giving words heal my troubled spirit and strengthen and restore my faith in our Almighty God. It was to me, the Great Physician daily doling out the exact dose of medicine needed to soothe a soul sickened, saddened, and disillusioned by rampant sinfulness. Each Psalm did in fact become precious; more precious than thousands of pieces of silver and gold.

In each Psalm, one key verse or phrase is selected that casts light on the entire meaning of the Psalm. A New Testament verse is shared that further illuminates the truth, thus demonstrating the continuity and oneness of the Bible; the weaving throughout of the story of the redemptive work of Jesus Christ. For the New is in the Old concealed and the Old is in the New revealed. I am continually inspired by the work of G. Campbell Morgan and his book, my long-time companion in Bible study, *Life Applications from Every Chapter of the Bible*.

Let the Word of Christ dwell in you richly. Colossians 3:16a

Author Note: The titles of each Psalm entry are the author's and focus the reader on the overall theme emphasized.

At the end of each Psalm entry are blank lines for the reader. The reader is encouraged to:

Record your own pleading and praising.
Write out the verses from the Psalm that you most treasure.
Share with someone who needs encouraged today.

Psalm 1: Like a Tree

Focus Verse:	New Testament Verse:
He is like a tree planted by streams of water, which yields its fruit in season and whose leaf does not wither. Whatever he does prospers. (3)	If a man remains in me and I in him, he will bear much fruit; apart from me you can do nothing. John 15:5

This, the first Psalm in the first of the five books of Psalms, the Genesis book, is among the most highly treasured of Psalms. I regularly find its life-giving phrases running through my mind and overflowing from my heart.

Because of the means devised, the sacrifice of Jesus Christ, I am no longer bound to:

❖ Walk in the counsel of the wicked
❖ Stand in the way of sinners
❖ Sit in the seat of mockers

Instead, because the "Word became flesh and dwelt among us" (John 1:14), I am able to delight in that Word, meditating on it day and night, being nurtured by that Word as my roots dig deep into its soil. Thus I am ever sustained, overflowing with joy, love, hope, happiness (blessings), and fruitfulness as I am able, through His presence, to live my life rightly.

But it is a daily, if not moment by moment, decision regarding how I spend my time, with whom I associate, what I allow to fill my mind and influence my thoughts. How gradually and subtly one can become seduced into deluded thinking. First listening to the advice of the supposedly worldly wise, then bit by bit acting more and more like them as one allows the world to squeeze one into its mold, until finally God is edged out of all thoughts and decisions, and one ultimately becomes fully antagonistic to God, mocking Him and denying His role in our daily lives and even His very existence.

The best way to discern falsehood is to be thoroughly grounded in the truth. Like the bank teller who learns to detect counterfeit bills, not by looking at counterfeits but by studying the genuine bill. The beautiful verse in Paul's letter to the Philippians comes to mind: *Finally, brothers, whatever is true, whatever is noble, whatever is right, whatever is pure, whatever is lovely, whatever is admirable–if anything is excellent or praiseworthy–think about these things (Phil. 4:8).*

Prayer:
Father, in a world where right and wrong are increasingly confused, You make it clear. May I let Your Word dwell in me richly so I will never get confused between right and wrong, so that I can live a beautiful and fruitful life that honors You. May I serve as a desperately needed oasis of green in a dry parched land. Apart from You, I can do nothing.

Psalm 2: It is All in Vain!

Focus Verse:	New Testament Verse:
Why do the nations conspire and the peoples plot in vain? (1)	that at the name of Jesus every knee should bow, in heaven and on earth and under the earth, and every tongue confess that Jesus Christ is Lord, to the glory of God the Father.
	Philippians 2:10, 11

People and nations conspire, plot, take their stand, and gather together against the Lord and against His Anointed One.

        IT   IS   ALL   IN   VAIN.

Through all the discouraging news cycles, the confusing conversations, the deluded thinking I am exposed to every day, because Jesus lives and triumphs over death and sin, "I will proclaim the decree of the Lord" (v. 7). The truths laid out in this Psalm yet remain even if they are not now acknowledged.

Jesus, the Anointed One, God's Son:
- ❖ Has been installed as King
- ❖ Has inherited all the nations
- ❖ Owns the entire earth
- ❖ Rules with an iron scepter
- ❖ Ultimately will destroy all wickedness

        JESUS   IS   LORD.

Blessed are those who take refuge in Him (v. 12).

The day is coming when Jesus will rise from that throne and return to Earth. Every eye in that moment will see Him as He is; every knee shall bow and every tongue

Janice Stauffer MacLeod

confess that He is Lord. As He lifts up His scepter, all those who have faithfully offered every part of themselves as instruments of righteous (Rom. 6:13) will join in a song of glorious, beautiful, and triumphant praise.

Prayer:
Thank You for reminding me again of who You are. Might I have the courage to proclaim You in a world that does not welcome You. May I faithfully offer every part of me to You as Your instruments of righteousness to use as You please that Your kingdom may come and Your will be done **even today**, on Earth, as it is in heaven.

_____
_____
_____
_____
_____
_____
_____
_____
_____

Psalm 3: Confidence

Focus Verse:	New Testament Verse:
Many are saying of me, "God will not deliver him." (2)	So we say with confidence, "The Lord is my helper; I will not be afraid. What can man do to me?"
	Hebrews 13:6

This is a Psalm written by David when he was fleeing the City of David-Jerusalem-when his own son Absalom rebelled against him and even his own men betrayed him. It is hard to imagine a lower moment, and easy to understand why even those closest to David concluded this time, God would not deliver him.

The King James Version says it well: "Lord, how are they increased that trouble me! Many are they that rise up against me!"

Though I am not facing the loss of a kingdom and am not in the sort of political trouble and family discord that King David experienced, I can certainly say as he did that those that trouble me are greatly increased. All I must do is turn on the news, engage in a conversation, or walk down the street.

But, despite the number of those that trouble me and their claims against my God, these truths remain, whether accepted by others or not:

- ❖ You are a shield around me, O Lord
- ❖ You bestow glory on me and lift my head
- ❖ You answer my cry from Your holy hill
- ❖ You sustain me through the night despite all that are drawn against me

- ❖ You will arise, You will deliver, You will destroy all wickedness
- ❖ From You alone comes salvation and blessing.

Prayer:
Father, thank You for Your protection. Thank You, that even in the midst of the most difficult adversity that many of my fellow believers are experiencing in various places all over the world (persecution, imprisonment, being ostracized by their own families, workplaces, and communities for their faith in You), You bestow Your glory on Your children and lift up their heads. You hear, You answer, You perfectly provide all that we need. You are our joy and our salvation. We can go to sleep at night and wake up the next morning, rested and confident that You are still in control. We pray with confidence, "The Lord is my helper; I will not be afraid. What can man do to me?" (Hebrews 13:6)

Psalm 4: Dealing With Anger

Focus Verse:	New Testament Verse:
In your anger do not sin; when you are on your beds, search your hearts and be silent. (4)	It [love] is not easily angered, it keeps no record of wrongs. 1 Corinthians 13:5 (b)

Anger, if not controlled, can be a problem. While there is much to justifiably be angry about, it is important, in the heat of that anger, to not give sin reign. Instead of letting anger be consuming, it is important to turn the anger into a time of soul searching, contemplation, and being still and silent in order to listen and hear God's voice directing in the right steps to take and healing words to say. In so doing, we allow His life-giving Word to richly nourish us, strengthen us, cleanse us, and comfort us. God's Word alone is truth and can teach us the way to take.

In *The Silver Chair*, one of the *Chronicles of Narnia* by CS Lewis, the Lion King Aslan carefully instructs the character Jill on four important signs she is to look for in order to be properly directed in the task she and her companions are assigned (Lewis, 1953). The third of four signs was to look for writing in stone in a ruined city and follow its directions. When stumbling around in the ruins of the city, right over and through the letters in the midst of a snowstorm, in a hurry to get to a castle they could see lighted and welcoming ahead of them, all three of the traveling companions failed to recognize the letters. Only later, looking down on the ruins from their vantage point in the castle, could they clearly see the lettering spelling out the instructions "UNDER ME." By then it was too late; the third sign, like the two proceeding, had been "miffed," as Jill described it.

I often think of this story and feel like I too am often stumbling about in the big "E" much like Jill and her companions, all the time missing the obvious signs around me (not unlike missing the forest for the trees).

Prayer:

Open my eyes, Father, that I might see things increasingly from Your perspective and less from my own limited view so that I see things as they truly are. Might I then willingly offer right sacrifices (my right to get angry at my circumstances) and simply trust in the Lord to, in the right way and in the right time, avenge on my behalf. Father please let the light of Your face shine upon me so that even though I am troubled, I may lie down and sleep in peace, for You alone, O Lord, make me dwell in safety.

_____
_____
_____
_____
_____
_____
_____
_____

Psalm 5: A Day of Danger

Focus Verse:	New Testament Verse:
In the morning, O LORD, you hear my voice; in the morning I lay my requests before You and wait in expectation. (3)	... offer yourselves to God, as those who have been brought from death to life; and offer the parts of your body to him as instruments of righteousness. Romans 6:13

G Campbell Morgan describes Psalm 5 as a prayer for a day of danger and suggests this translation of the selected verse, "O Lord in the morning shalt Thou hear my voice; in the morning will I order . . . unto Thee and will keep watch" (Morgan, 1994).

Since all days are potential days of danger, it is important to daily prepare by:

- ❖ Worship: remembering who we are-and whose we are-to keep a correct perspective of the situation faced
- ❖ Order (arrange): that is, prayerfully preparing-now with a right perspective from worshiping in spirit and in truth
- ❖ Wait: keeping a vigilant watch (all day), not only to be alert to His actions on our behalf, but also to monitor our own fear-driven tendencies to be led astray or to taking premature action, thus disregarding the careful and prayerful Spirit-led preparation

Prayer:
Father, as I worship You each new day, may I then prayerfully prepare for the day by offering all of me to You as instruments of righteousness so that all I think, see, hear,

speak, do, and where I go will be in accordance with Your good, pleasing, and perfect will. Please lead me by Your righteousness as I wait in watchful expectation for Your working out Your perfect will in my life.

___
___
___
___
___
___
___
___

Psalm 6: A Long Way Off

Focus Verse:	New Testament Verse:
The LORD has heard my cry for mercy; the LORD accepts my prayer. (9)	But while he was a long way off, his father saw him and was filled with compassion for him; he ran to his son, threw his arms around him and kissed him. Luke 15:20

We all want to be heard and accepted. With God, we can count on the truth, that our prayers pleading for His mercy will always be heard and accepted. How beautiful this is. How illustrative of the tender mercies of our loving God, who, when a guilty, desperate soul in anguish cries out to his God, immediately turns to deliver, to save with His unfailing love, and to hear and accept back richly. Much like the father in the gospel parable who ran with eagerness and joy to greet his wayward (prodigal) *but returning* son when he was still a long way off (Luke 15:20).

It seems I want Him least when I need Him most, for I have been a long way off. But it is in that recognition of our condition, the decision to turn back toward home, the overwhelming realization of our need for deliverance (again), our crying out, that we find our God is ever ready to forgive, heal, and richly restore. And is, in fact, running to meet us.

Prayer:
Thank You, Lord, for hearing my cry for mercy. Thank You for accepting my prayer. For though I am still a long

way off, I am headed back to You. I can see You running to meet me, for You have never left me.

_____
_____
_____
_____
_____
_____
_____
_____

Psalm 7: A God Who Sees and Acts

Focus Verse:	New Testament Verse:
O LORD my God, I take refuge in you; save and deliver me from all who pursue me, (1)	Let us hold unswervingly to the hope we profess, for he who promised is faithful. Hebrews 10:23

David, having been falsely accused of wrongdoing by Saul, the King of Israel, turns to his Lord God for refuge and deliverance, pleading with God to "judge me according to my integrity"; "to rise up against the rage of my enemies; to awake and decree justice" (v. 6).
David knew his God well, thus turning to Him in this situation in utter confidence. David knew:

- God is a God of justice and righteousness
- God searches minds and hearts and judges according to what He sees (David had nothing to hide)
- God will decree justice, bringing an end to the violence of the wicked, making the righteous secure and saving the upright in heart

Of all the attributes of God, I am most thankful that my God is a God of justice. I am also thankful that He is a God who sees and searches and that He is a God who acts. We live in a world where evil and injustice are rampant, where false accusations abound. Because of this, the believer must take special care, as David did, to live a life above reproach, especially toward those who are our enemies, thus giving them no ammunition for accusations. When, in spite of this, false accusations are hurled, the person of integrity can yet expect the God of justice to ultimately triumph, in His good time.

Prayer:
Father, I thank You that You are a God who sees, who searches, who judges with justice, and rules in righteousness. I thank You that You are a God of action who will bring an end to the violence and false accusations of the wicked, thus making the righteous secure (v. 17). Help me to patiently wait for Your perfect timing.

Psalm 8: A Visited People

Focus Verse:	New Testament Verse:
What is man that thou are mindful of him? and the son of man that thou visitest him? (4) KJV	Blessed be the Lord God of Israel; for he hath visited and redeemed his people. Luke 1:68 (KJV)

The most beautiful truth in the Bible is that God chose to "visit" our world. He cared so much that He chose to become *"flesh and dwell among us"* (John 1:14). He stooped down to make us great, shattering the heavens to come down to our level so we could behold His glory (Ps. 18). He made His light shine out of the darkness into our hearts to give us the light of the knowledge of the glory of God in the face of Christ. We are made capable of beholding His majesty through Jesus (2 Cor. 4)!

Prayer:
I, like the psalmist, stand amazed. "What is man that Thou are mindful of him?" In spite of the wonder of all of Your creation in all its vast array, You still are mindful of man, caring for him and crowing him with glory and honor. In all Your heavenly majesty and glory, You choose to use the praise from the lips of children to silence Your enemies, foes, and the avenger. Father, thank You for sending Your Son Jesus to visit and redeem us so that we might know You.

Psalm 9: Pleading and Praising

Focus Verse:	New Testament Verse:
He will judge the world in righteousness; he will govern the peoples with justice (8).	His divine power has given us everything we need for a godly life through our knowledge of him who called us by his own glory and goodness. Through these he has given us his very great and precious promises, so that through them you may participate in the divine nature, having escaped the corruption in the world caused by evil desires.
	2 Peter 1:3, 4

This Psalm of David is a heartfelt mingling of praise and pleading as the psalmist finds his footing on the promises of His God.

The promises:
- ❖ The Lord, the judge of the world, is known by His justice. He is:
    - o A refuge for the oppressed
    - o A stronghold in times of trouble
    - o An upholder of the right
- ❖ He has never forsaken those who seek Him
- ❖ He who avenges blood *remembers* and does not ignore the cry of the afflicted

The Pleas:
- ❖ See how my enemies persecute me!
- ❖ Have mercy on me and lift me from the gates of death
- ❖ Do not let men triumph; let the nations know they are but men

Janice Stauffer MacLeod

- Judge the nations in Your presence

The Praise:
- I will tell of Your wonders; I will be glad and rejoice in You
- You have upheld my right and my cause, judging righteously
- The wicked who reject the Lord end up being ensnared by the works of their own hands
- My enemies turn back, stumbling and perishing before You
- You have rebuked the nations and destroyed the wicked, blotting out their name forever; their cites uprooted to the point that their very memory has perished
- You reign forever and have established Your throne for judgment
- You judge in righteousness and govern with justice

It is only when we as individuals, and collectively as nations, see ourselves as we truly are in God's sight that we, in realizing our fragility, wickedness, and hopelessness, can then turn and be healed, rescued, and restored by the just and righteous Judge of all the earth.

Prayer:
Father, thank You for the great and precious promises that allow us not only to escape the corruption in the world caused by evil desires, but to participate in the divine nature, right now!

Psalm 10: Asking Tough Questions

Focus Verse:	New Testament Verse:
In his pride the wicked does not seek him; in all his thoughts there is no room for God. (4)	"It is mine to avenge; I will repay," says the Lord. Romans 12:19b

The troubled psalmist cries out to his God, "Why, O Lord, do you stand far off? Why do you hide yourself in times of trouble?"

Though for a season (that often feels interminably long to us) the wicked man escapes God's notice, gets away with and prospers, despite his:

- ❖ Arrogant hunting down of the weak
- ❖ Devious and deceitful schemes
- ❖ Boastings, cravings, and greed
- ❖ Pride and inflated ego (edging God out until there is no room for Him)
- ❖ Haughtiness, disregard for God's laws, his perceived invincibility, and confidence
- ❖ Curses, lies, and threats
- ❖ Ambushing of the innocent and helpless

The truth-seeking psalmist yet remembers and realizes anew that his God is, in fact:

- ❖ Near (not far off and not in hiding)
- ❖ He does hear, remember, see, and consider
- ❖ He will lift His hand and He will arise to help and encourage all who commit themselves to Him

> The wicked man will terrify no more.

To answer the psalmist's (and our) opening question: the King of kings, our God, is near; He is not hiding; He sees, hears, remembers, considers, arises, lifts His hand, helps the helpless, and calls the wicked to account.

Prayer:
Thank You, Heavenly Father, that all of this is true. These are promises that we can stand on, for You have spoken them.

_____
_____
_____
_____
_____
_____
_____
_____

Psalm 11: When Up is Down

Focus Verse:	New Testament Verse:
When the foundations are being destroyed what can the righteous do? (3)	And we all, who with unveiled faces contemplate the Lord's glory, are being transformed into his likeness with ever-increasing glory, which comes from the Lord, who is the Spirit. 2 Corinthians 3:18

We live in a world of turmoil in which the very foundations that have made this nation great are being seriously eroded to the point of utter destruction. What was right is now labeled wrong; what was wrong is now labeled right; up is down and down is up. All is true, yet nothing is true, for truth is seen to be relative and in the eyes of the beholder, varying from day to day or even hour by hour for the same person. The solid foundation that truth provided no longer exists for many. How can a believer live in such a shifting world? In the words of the psalmist, "what can the righteous do?"

The response: "The Lord is in his holy temple; the Lord is on his heavenly throne" (v. 4).

The wicked have indeed destroyed their very foundation by utterly trampling on and mocking the truth. The house of cards of the wicked will ultimately collapse in a storm of fiery coals, burning sulfur, and scorching wind. Yet, for the righteous, their foundation, the rock-solid Word of the Lord remains strong and steadfast, for the Lord is yet in His holy temple; He yet sits on His heavenly throne. Our Lord yet reigns triumphant over sin and death.

The Lord, our Lord, the Lord on the throne, is righteous. He loves justice. He promises us that upright men will see His face (v. 7). We who are upright are so by the grace of our loving Lord, who exchanged the filthy rags of our righteousness for His own royal robes. The Lord on His throne observes and examines. When He looks at His own, He increasingly sees the likeness of His Son Jesus Christ being reflected in our now unveiled faces as we reflect His glory.

Prayer:
Father, when I consider all this: when friends disappoint me, when the world around me seems to be disintegrating into chaos, remind me to look up and to see You in all Your majesty on Your throne, to gaze upon You in all Your beauty and holiness with an unveiled face so that I can increasingly reflect Your glory to a battered and blinded world.

Psalm 12: Holding Out the Word of Truth

Focus Verse:	New Testament Verse:
And the words of the LORD are flawless, like silver refined in a furnace of clay, purified seven times. (6)	so that you may become blameless and pure, children of God without fault in a crooked and depraved generation in which you shine like stars in the universe as you hold out the word of life.
	Philippians 2:15, 16a

In this Psalm, David, the psalmist, describes a godless world from which the faithful have vanished, where everyone lies to his neighbor, their flattering lips speak deception and their proud lips declare triumph as the wicked strut about while what is vile is honored. He could well be describing our world today.

As amazing as it may be, in this world, God's Word stands as a firm foundation; a bright light, flawless, refined, and purified. Regardless of the desperateness of the circumstances, in His perfect timing, the Lord will arise; He will protect and keep safe those who trust in Him.

It is in this world that God is counting on us, His children, to keep ourselves blameless and pure, without fault in a crooked and depraved generation so we can shine like untarnished stars in the universe as we offer to all His life-giving Word. Jesus Himself, on the night of His crucifixion, specifically prayed for us in regards to this task: *I have given them your word and the world has hated them, for they are not of the world. My prayer is not that you take them out of the world but that you protect them from the evil one.*

They are not of the world, even as I am not of it. Sanctify them by the truth; your word is truth (John 17:14-17).

Prayer:
Father, show me opportunities to share Your Word, to hold it out to an increasingly desperate world. If I am to share Your Word, I must be reading through Your Word, praying in Your Word, and faithfully living out Your Word in consistent, continual, complete, and immediate obedience. Then, I can, with confidence and with love, stand up for and proclaim Your truth at any cost. How badly the world today needs Your flawless, refined, and purified Word. May I be faithful to the task. May my fellow believers around the globe be encouraged, knowing Jesus Himself prayed specifically for us on the last night of His earthly ministry that we might be equipped for this task.

_____
_____
_____
_____
_____
_____
_____
_____

Psalm 13: The Translator

Focus Verse:	New Testament Verse:
How long…? (1, 2)	In the same way, the Spirit helps us in our weakness. We do not know what we ought to pray for, but the Spirit himself intercedes for us with groans that words cannot express. And he who searches our hearts knows the mind of the Spirit, because the Spirit intercedes for the saints in accordance with God's will.
	Romans 8:26, 27

In this Psalm, we learn something of the purpose and the power of prayer of a man after God's heart, as the psalmist David is known to be.

The Psalm opens (vv. 1-2) with David questioning his God, "How long":

- ❖ Will You forget me, forever?
- ❖ Will You hide Yourself from me?
- ❖ Must I wrestle with my thoughts and everyday have sorrow in my heart?
- ❖ Will my enemy triumph over me?

David demands answers of his God, desperately pleading for light for his eyes so he can avoid death and his enemy's gloating over him when he is overcome and falls (vv. 3-4).

Suddenly, David's tone changes as he ends his prayer: *But I trust in your unfailing love; my heart rejoices in your salvation. I will sing to the Lord, for He has been good to me* (vv. 5-6).

Though David's circumstances have not changed, as he poured out his heart, his view of God did change and thus he progressed from the despair of the first four verses of this Psalm to end with words of rejoicing and song. As we come into our God's presence with our complaints, our honest contemplations, and our true confessions, this allows the eyes of our hearts to be opened and enlightened (Eph. 1:18) so that we may see through our earthly circumstances to His glorious unfailing love and precious salvation. Thus, as for David, our complaints transition to praise, rejoicing, thanksgiving, and singing.

Prayer:
Father, You have taught us to pray. You, who know our hearts, have promised through Your Spirit within us, that You will take our troubled words and translate them into the perfect petition so that soon, our pleading turns to praise. Thank You that You always hear (and translate) our prayers. Thank You that the Spirit ever intercedes for us in accordance with Your good, pleasing, and perfect will. I must simply come into Your presence.

Psalm 14: Suppressing the Truth

Focus Verse:	New Testament Verse:
The LORD looks down from heaven on the sons of men to see if there are any who understand, any who seek God. (2)	for all have sinned and fall short of the glory of God, Romans 3:23

In searching, the Lord finds all have turned aside, they have together become corrupt; there is no one who does good, not even one (v. 3). Instead, the psalmist laments that we are all living and acting like the fool who says *in his heart*, "There is no God" (v. 1).

The Hebrew word for "fool" that is used in this Psalm refers to wickedness rather than limited intellect. The atheist that desires *in his heart* (as described here) to be rid of God, that denies His rule and His intervention in one's life, inevitably is led into wickedness. By contrast, the agnostic has not shut the door to the potential truth of the existence of an almighty God, but has not yet found evidence of this. G. Campbell Morgan shares a thought-provoking perspective regarding this Psalm: "It is possible for a man to yield himself so completely to desire, as to be able to persuade himself that he really does believe what he wants to believe, and thus to set his will free for all evil choices" (Morgan, 1994).

Consider Romans 1. An obedience that comes from faith is described. In contrast, the wickedness of men who *suppress the truth* leads to futile thinking; foolish, darkened hearts; a surrender to the sinful desires of their hearts; the exchange of the truth of God for a lie; and a depraved mind leading to ever-escalating wickedness, evil, and greed, ultimately resulting in approval of those around them who also practice the same depravity.

Father, just as in the times of Noah, how grieved, how filled with pain Your heart must be to see how great man's wickedness on the earth has become; to find that every inclination of the thoughts of his heart are only evil all the time (Gen. 6:5-6). Yet, it was into this very world that You chose to come, dying for us while we were yet sinners.

Prayer:

Thank You that in recognizing our utter failure, when every single one of us has fallen far short of Your glory, You provided the gift of eternal life through Christ Jesus our Lord (Rom. 6:23). You devised a way that we might not remain estranged from You. Fill us with the faith that leads to obedience; rid us of the wickedness that suppresses the truth. Lead us not into temptation but deliver us from evil.

_____
_____
_____
_____
_____
_____
_____
_____

Psalm 15: Going to the Heights

Focus Verse:	New Testament Verse:
Lord, who may dwell in your sanctuary? Who may live on your holy hill?	For this reason, since the day we heard about you, we have not stopped praying for you and asking God to fill you with the knowledge of his will through all spiritual wisdom and understanding. And we pray this in order that you may live a life worthy of the Lord and may please him in every way; bearing fruit in every good work, growing in the knowledge of God, being strengthened with all power according to his glorious might so that you may have great endurance and patience, and joyfully giving thanks to the Father, who has qualified you to share in this inheritance of the saints in the kingdom of light. Colossians 1:9-12

This Psalm by David lists the qualifications of the one who may dwell in the sanctuary of the Lord:

❖ He whose walk is blameless and who does what is righteous (grace gives us the ability to choose not to sin; Father, I offer my hands and feet to be Your hands and feet so that what I do and where I go is in accordance to Your good, pleasing, and perfect will)

❖ Who speaks the truth from his heart and has no slander on his tongue (may I take time to listen to You each day so I can hear as You give to me words of wisdom and healing that I might know the word to sustain the weary)

❖ Who does his neighbor no wrong and casts no slur on his fellowman (instead of finding fault with my spouse, my coworker, my neighbor, the unknown individuals I encounter in my day, may I be a source of encouragement to all paths I cross today, leaving Your footprints of grace in my wake)

- ❖ Who despises a vile man but honors those who fear the Lord (help me stand up for the truth and in defense of the disadvantaged at all costs today)
- ❖ Who keeps his oath even when it hurts (help me to keep my word today)
- ❖ Who lends his money without usury and does not accept a bribe against the innocent (help me to see opportunities to share my-Your-resources with those in need today)

God promises that those who do these things will never be shaken. How badly our world needs more such stable people. May I, through God's help, be one of them.

Rereading David's opening question consider the words of the prophet Habakkuk years later, "The Sovereign Lord is my strength, he makes my feet like the feet of a deer, he enables me to go on the heights" (Hab. 3:19).

Prayer:
Father, with Your presence living and working through me, all this is possible. Without Your presence, it is impossible. Enable me to go on the heights that I might dwell in Your sanctuary.

Psalm 16: Contentment

Focus Verse:	New Testament Verse:
I said to the LORD, "You are my Lord; apart from you I have no good thing." (2)	I have learned to be content whatever the circumstances. I know what it is to be in need, and I know what it is to have plenty. I have learned the secret of being content in any and every situation, whether well fed or hungry, whether living in plenty or in want. Philippians 4:11, 12

Only the one who has truly accepted His Lordship as our Messiah, ever about his Father's business, regularly in deep communion with Him, speaking and doing only His perfect will, can truly sacrifice "all the vain things that charm me most" to His throne. One this surrendered:

- ❖ Delights in the fellowship of other believers
- ❖ Realizes the futility and ultimate sorrow of those who run after other gods
- ❖ Is fully contented regardless of circumstances, recognizing the soul in communion with its God dwells in a pleasant place and has in store a delightful inheritance
- ❖ Is continually attentive to the Lord's counsel and instruction day and night
- ❖ Ever has the Lord before him and thus nothing shakes him
- ❖ Is glad, ever-rejoicing, rests secure, realizing the Lord has revealed the Way, the Truth, and the Life eternal in His presence forevermore.

Prayer:
Father, I pray as did David, You are my Lord; apart from You I have no good thing (v. 2). With You, the boundary lines have fallen for me in pleasant places; surely I have a delightful inheritance (v. 6). You have made known to me the path of life; You will fill me with joy in Your presence, with eternal pleasures at Your right hand (v. 11).

_____
_____
_____
_____
_____
_____
_____

Psalm 17: Seeing His Face

Focus Verse:	New Testament Verse:
And I–in righteousness, I will see your face; when I awake, I will be satisfied with seeing your likeness. (15)	Blessed are the pure in heart for they will see God. Matthew 5:8

David is struggling to live in a way that honors God in a world that is determined to dishonor Him. It is a world of violence, wickedness, and vindictiveness. Yet David remains steadfast in his devotion to his God; his deepest desire is to see his God in all His righteousness and to increasingly reflect that righteousness in his own life, despite the rampant evil working against him at every turn. Thus he turns to his God for His ever-present help.

David's prayer:
- ❖ Hear my righteous pleas
- ❖ Listen
- ❖ Give ear
- ❖ Vindicate
- ❖ See
- ❖ Probe
- ❖ Examine
- ❖ Test
- ❖ Answer
- ❖ Show Your love
- ❖ Save
- ❖ Keep
- ❖ Hide

- ❖ Rise up and bring down my enemies whose reward is in this life

How apt David's prayer is for believers today who, like David, find themselves struggling to live in a way that honors God in a world determined to dishonor Him. How do we live in a Romans 1 world? We faithfully spend time in the Almighty's presence, seeking His help, guidance, will, and ways.

Prayer:

Father, thank You for Your precious promise, taught by Jesus Himself in His Sermon on the Mount, "Blessed are the pure in heart, for they will see God." Father, thank You for patiently working in my life to make me pure in heart. Thank You for opening the eyes of my heart that I might see You in all Your righteousness.

Psalm 18: He Stooped Down

Focus Verse:	New Testament Verse:
He parted the heavens and came down ...(9)	The Word became flesh and made his dwelling among us. We have seen his glory, the glory of the One and Only, who came from the Father, full of grace and truth.
	John 1:14

This is David's song to the Lord when delivered from his enemies, with the cords and snares of death entangling and confronting him and with torrents of destruction overwhelming him.

This is our song to the Lord when delivered from our enemies, like David, with the cords of sin and death and destruction entangling, overwhelming, and confronting us ...

The Lord saved me; it is completed (note the past tense)
I called to the Lord (v. 6)
From his temple he heard my voice (v. 6)
He parted the heavens and came down (v. 9)
He shot his arrows and scattered, routed, and exposed the enemies (v. 14)
He reached down from on high and took hold of me (v. 16)
He rescued me from my powerful enemy (v. 17)
He brought me into a spacious place (v. 19)

I am being sanctified; it is being done (note the present tense)
He keeps my lamp burning, turning darkness into light (v. 28)
He arms me with strength (v. 32)
He makes my way perfect (v. 32)

He makes my feet like the feet of a deer (v. 33)
He enables me to stand on the heights (v. 33)
He trains my hands for battle (v. 34)
He gives me the shield of victory (v. 35)
His right hand sustains me (v. 35)
He stoops down to make me great (v. 35)
He broadens the path beneath me (v. 36)
The Lord lives! Praise be to my Rock! (v. 46)
Exalted be God my Savior! (v. 46)
He shows unfailing kindness to his anointed (v. 50).

Prayer:
Father, of all that You do for me, I am most grateful that You, despite Your majesty and glory, chose to shatter the heavens, *to stoop down to my level*, to make me great. Thank You, Lord, for becoming flesh and dwelling among us so we could *be saved* and we *can continually behold and reflect Your glory right now!*

_____
_____
_____
_____
_____
_____
_____
_____

Psalm 19: The Heavens Declare His Glory

Focus Verse:	New Testament Verse:
The heavens declare the glory of God; the skies proclaim the work of his hands (1).	For since the creation of the world God's invisible qualities–His eternal power and divine nature–have been clearly seen, being understood from what has been made, so that men are without excuse. Romans 1:20

Day after day, the heavens declare the glory of God and proclaim the work of His hands; night after night, they display knowledge. In fact, all the way to the ends of the earth, there is no speech or language or place where their voice is not heard. Nowhere!

Once, when Abram (not yet Abraham) was deeply discouraged and doubting God's amazing promises to him, the Word of the Lord came to him in a vision, assuring Abram of the certainness of His great plan, and that in spite of Abram's advanced age and childless condition, he would become the father of many nations. As an object lesson he would never forget, the Lord took Abram outside and told him to "look up at the heaven and count the stars-if indeed you can count them. So shall your offspring be." The Bible records Abram believed the Lord and He credited it to him as righteousness (Gen. 15:1-6). When we are deeply discouraged, doubting, disappointed, defeated, disillusioned, desperate even, then is a good time to go outside on a clear, bright, starry night and simply "look up…"

Look up, look up to the heavens; behold His glory...
Then, with a fresh perspective, look deeply into His life-giving Word. Read every precious promise again as if for the first time...
For His Word is:
- ❖ Perfect → Reviving the soul
- ❖ Trustworthy → Making wise the simple
- ❖ Right → Giving joy to the heart
- ❖ Radiant → Giving light to the eyes
- ❖ Pure → Enduring forever
- ❖ Sure and altogether righteous → By them is Your servant warned
- ❖ Precious and sweet → In keeping it, there is great reward

Prayer:
May the words of my mouth and the meditations of my heart be pleasing in your sight, O Lord, my Rock and my Redeemer (v. 14).

_____
_____
_____
_____
_____
_____
_____
_____

Psalm 20: Chariot Trusters

Some trust in chariots and some in horses; but we trust in the name of the LORD our God (7)	Therefore put on the full armor of God, so that when the day of evil comes, you may be able to stand your ground, and after you have done everything, to stand.
	Ephesians 6:13

As I read this Psalm of David, I consider the possible challenges for David and his armies. We do not know for sure the exact circumstances, but can certainly point to many extraordinary situations that David faced over the years. What about my own situation? What challenges do I face today? What about my fellow believers, both down the street and around the globe? What if these words became our own, regardless of our circumstances?

What is evident in this Psalm is an absolute confidence in the faithfulness and capability of his God in providing not just protection from the enemy, but overwhelming victory and triumph. G. Campbell Morgan states in regards to this Psalm, "Faith has only one anxiety and that is to be found ranged on the side of God. When that is so, it can know no fear" (Morgan, 1994).

David contrasts those who trust in chariots (that is earthly, materialistic things) versus those who trust in the name of the Lord (God trusters).

Chariot trusters are brought to their knees, disappearing in the swirl of the Red Sea waters, returning to their rightful place. God trusters rise and miraculously march between walls of water in the middle of a sea by the saving power of God's right hand. Chariot trusters are bowed down and fallen while God trusters are risen, and stand upright (v. 8).

How is this possible? A New Testament passage (Eph. 6:10-18) describes what it takes:

God trusters:
- ❖ Are strong in the Lord and in His mighty power, thus can stand their ground against the day of evil
- ❖ Put on the full armor of God so they can take their stand against the devil's schemes (the belt of truth, the breastplate of righteousness, feet fitted with the readiness of the gospel of peace, the shield of faith, the helmet of salvation, the sword of the Spirit, and prayer)
- ❖ Recognize the struggle is not against flesh and blood (therefore chariots and horses are useless) but against rulers, authorities, powers of this dark world, and the spiritual forces of evil in the heavenly realm.

Prayer:
O Lord, save us! Answer us when we call! Help us to be prepared for what today will bring by recognizing our strength is ever and always in You.

Psalm 21: Steadfastness

Focus Verse:	New Testament Verse:
For the king trusts in the LORD; through the unfailing love of the Most High, he will not be shaken. (7	Now faith is being sure of what we hope for and certain of what we do not see.
	Hebrews 11:1
	By faith, Abraham, even though he was past age–and Sarah herself was barren–was enabled to become a father because he considered him faithful who had made the promise.
	Hebrews 11:11
	All these people were still living by faith when they died. They did not receive the things promised; they only saw them and welcomed them from a distance. And they admitted that they were aliens and strangers on earth.
	Hebrews 11:13

This is the secret to national and personal success; an unswerving trust in the Lord, the Most High, and His unfailing love. The result is steadfastness, strength, eternal life, victory, splendor, and majesty as the believer increasingly reflects the Lord's radiance, gladness, and joy. And thus the wicked are foiled and none of the evil plotting or devious schemes will ultimately succeed.

Do I exalt the Lord in my daily life? Am I victorious, praising His strength and might? Do I rejoice in all He has done for me? Or do I project discouragement, uncertainty, even fear?

I must remember Abram's object lesson. When discouraged, defeated, dismayed, disillusioned, even desperate, I must look up to the stars and remember who He is: the Almighty Creator of all things; the great Deliverer. Then I must look deep into His Word and remember and declare His glorious promises. Like Abram, later Abraham, I can know for certain His promises will all be fulfilled, down to the last detail, even if now I am seeing them from a distance (Gen. 15).

Prayer:
Father, give me a faith that is sure of what I hope for and certain of what I do not yet see (Heb. 11:1).

Psalm 22 (A Messianic Psalm): It is Finished

Focus Verse:	New Testament Verse:
They will proclaim his righteousness to a people yet unborn–for he has done it. (31)	"It is finished." John 19:30

The Messiah:
- ❖ Was forsaken
- ❖ Was alone in the groaning and crying out
- ❖ Was a worm, scorned, mocked, and insulted (He trusts in the Lord; let the Lord rescue him. Let him deliver him, since he delights in him.)
- ❖ Was completely alone as strong bulls and roaring lions with mouths open wide surrounded him
- ❖ Was poured out like water with His bones all out of joint, His heart melted, and His tongue stuck to the roof of His mouth
- ❖ Was surrounded by a band of evil men who encircled Him, piercing His hands and feet
- ❖ Was stared at, gloated over, while His garments were divided

It was because of this that...
- ❖ Your name will be declared and praised
- ❖ You will be honored and revered
- ❖ The poor will eat and be satisfied
- ❖ All the ends of the earth will remember and turn to the Lord
- ❖ All the families of the nations will bow down before You, for dominion belongs to You

- ❖ All the riches of the earth will feast and worship
- ❖ All who die will kneel before You
- ❖ Future generations will be told about the Lord, proclaiming Your righteousness to future generations, for "IT IS FINISHED"

Prayer:
Messiah, thank You for suffering and dying on my behalf that I might live.

_____
_____
_____
_____
_____
_____
_____

Psalm 23: I Shall Not Want

Focus Verse:	New Testament Verse:
The Lord is my shepherd, I shall not be in want. (1)	Our Father, which art in heaven... Matthew 6:9 (KJV)

The Lord is my Shepherd.
Because this is the case, I shall not be in want.
- ❖ He will guide and direct me in the best ways, whether it be:

Lying down in green pastures (feeding on Your Word)
Drinking deeply of Your life-giving water (the well of salvation)
Walking in paths of righteousness
- ❖ I am freed from fear and evil as He provides comfort and security
- ❖ My soul is restored as He gives me bountiful, overflowing blessings, hope, goodness, and love
- ❖ I will spend eternity in heaven with my Shepherd

The Lord is my Shepherd, the good Shepherd. He knows me and I know Him. He gave His life for me so I could live (John 10:11-15).

How beautifully the two most beloved prayers, one from the Old, and the other from the New (The Lord's Prayer, Matthew 6:9-13 KJV), are intertwined, each one itself complete:

The Lord is my Shepherd
    <Our Father which art in heaven>
I shall not be in want
He makes me lie down in green pastures
He leads me beside quiet waters
He restores my soul

<Give us this day our daily bread>
He guides me in paths of righteousness
<and lead us not into temptation>
For his name's sake
<Hallowed be your Name>
Even though I walk through the valley of the shadow of death, I will fear no evil, for you are with me
<But deliver us from evil>
Your rod and your staff, they comfort me
<and forgive us our debts as we forgive our debtors>
You prepare a table before me in the presence of my enemies; you anoint my head with oil; my cup overflows
<Thy kingdom come, Thy will be done, in Earth as it is in heaven>
Surely goodness and love will follow me all the days of my life and I will dwell in the house of the Lord forever.
<For Thine is the kingdom, the power, and the glory forever. Amen.>

Prayer:
Father, thank You for teaching us to pray.

_____
_____
_____
_____
_____
_____
_____
_____

Psalm 24: The King of Glory

Focus Verse:	New Testament Verse:
The earth is the LORD's and everything in it, the world and all who live in it; (1)	And I heard a loud voice from the throne saying, "Now the dwelling of God is with men, and he will live with them. They will be his people, and God himself will be with them and be their God. Revelation 21:3

He founded and established the earth. He, the Creator and Sustainer of all things, is altogether holy, high and lifted up, strong and mighty, the King of glory.
And yet, knowing all this, the psalmist dares to ask:
- ❖ Who may ascend to the hill of the Lord?
- ❖ Who may stand in His holy place?
- ❖ Who may receive blessings from the Lord and vindication from God his Savior?

The answer: only the seeker who:
- ❖ Has clean hands and a pure heart
- ❖ Does not lift his soul to an idol
- ❖ Does not swear by what is false

It is this very King of glory Himself who stoops down to make me great, who makes my feet like the feet of a deer, enabling me to stand on the heights!

Prayer:
I open the gates of my heart that You, my King of glory, may come in.

Psalm 25: Show Me Your Ways

Focus Verse:	New Testament Verse:
Show me Your ways, O LORD, teach me your paths, guide me in your truth, and teach me, for you are God my Savior, and my hope is in you all day long (4)	Jesus answered, "I am the way and the truth and the life. No one comes to the Father except through me." John 14:6

David is a soul in deep need as he cries out to his God in these verses. He is facing treacherous enemies that are increasing in number. He is reaping the results of his youthful rebellion and struggling with more recent iniquities that have ensnared him. He is wrestling with loneliness, affliction, troubles, and anguish. Yet, throughout his heartfelt petitions for the Lord's help, is woven an utter confidence in the ability and willingness of his Lord to rescue and redeem him. He reminds the Lord (and at the same time, himself) of His great mercy and love and goodness.

What a model for prayer this is for us. There can be no prayer the Lord longs more to answer than:

"Show me your ways, O Lord."

"Teach me your paths."

"Guide me in your truth."

"Teach me."

Reading on, we learn that even more than this:

The Lord confides in those who fear Him; He makes His covenant known to them (v. 14).

Prayer:
Father, when I have made shambles of things and my tendency might be to not talk to You because I am so ashamed of myself and disappointed in how I have once again failed You, may I, like David, turn my eyes to You, and keep my eyes on You, for it is You and You alone who can "release my feet from the snare" (v. 15). Once again, my merciful, loving, and good God, show me Your ways, teach me Your paths, guide me in Your truth, and teach me. I long to commune with You again, to have You confide in me and make Your covenant known. Jesus is the way.

_____

_____

_____

_____

_____

_____

_____

Psalm 26: Walking in the Truth

Focus Verse:	New Testament Verse:
for Your love is ever before me, and I walk continually in your truth. (3)	And I will ask the Father, and He will give you another Counselor to be with you forever–the Spirit of truth.
	John 14:16, 17a
	But when he, the Spirit of truth, comes, he will guide you into all truth.
	John 16:13

Like David, I live among deceitful, hypocritical, wicked, blood-thirsty, scheming, bribing sinners. The only way I can lead a blameless life in this environment is maintaining an unwavering trust in my loving and faithful Lord, walking continually in His truth, keeping in step with His Spirit, and then proclaiming aloud His praise, telling of His wonderful work on my behalf.

Why is it so hard to take a stand in a world gone mad? I often feel so confused, buffeted about-left speechless in amazement at all I witness.

Prayer:
But Father, You said this world would be a strange place for believers, for we are not of this world. But You also specifically chose to keep us in this world (John 17:15-16). You promised Your precious Holy Spirit to be our Counselor and Guide-to lead us into all truth. Your Word is true. Your promises are true. I am, in this moment, dwelling in Your love and walking in Your truth. For Your love is ever before me and I walk continually in Your truth (v. 3). How life-giving and healing is this truth.

Psalm 27: Remembering Who He is

Focus Verse:	New Testament Verse:
The LORD is my light and my salvation — whom shall I fear? The LORD is the stronghold of my life-of whom shall I be afraid? (1)	But seek first his kingdom and his righteousness and all these things will be given to you as well. Matthew 6:33

This is David's prayer in times of darkness, division, derision, deceit, despair, and defeat. It can be our prayer too when facing disturbing circumstances. We need not be disturbed by disturbances.

You, my Lord, are my:
- Light
- Salvation
- Stronghold
- Beauty
- Shelter
- Mercy
- Helper
- Teacher
- Leader
- Goodness

This is a prayer for protection from rampant evil. As in the Lord's prayer, "lead us not into temptation but deliver us from evil…"

Prayer:
Father, at times when I am in despair, I must, as David did, take time to remember who You are. I must spend time in Your presence, seeking Your face, gazing at Your

beauty and learning of Your ways. I must, like David, be strong, take heart, and wait for You. David, in spite of all the evil he witnessed, believed he would see Your goodness in the land of the living.

Father, help me seek You first.

Psalm 28: All Our Troubles

Focus Verse:	New Testament Verse:
To You I call, O LORD, my Rock; do not turn a deaf ear to me (1)	Praise be to the God and Father of our Lord Jesus Christ, the Father of compassion and the God of all comfort, who comforts us in all our troubles, so that we can comfort those in any trouble with the comfort we ourselves have received from God.
	2 Corinthians 1:3, 4

My Lord, Jehovah, My Rock, the Immutable:
- ❖ Who hears my call
- ❖ Who answers my plea
- ❖ Who in mercy comes to my aid
- ❖ Who works His perfect justice according to His holiness

My Lord is my fortress, my strength. He is my Rock. My Savior. My Shepherd. Forever.

I praise You, the Father of compassion and the God of all comfort, who comforts us in all our troubles.

All our troubles.

Even those of our own making.

Prayer:
Father, in considering all of this, my heart leaps for joy. May I allow the comfort You have brought to me regularly overflow from my life into the lives of others. In fact, maybe that is why we sometimes experience hardships. Thank You!

Psalm 29: A Strange Peace

Focus Verse:	New Testament Verse:
Ascribe to the LORD the glory due his name, worship the LORD in the splendor of his holiness. (2)	Peace I leave with you; my peace I give you. I do not give to you as the world gives. Do not let your hearts be troubled and do not be afraid.
Give unto the LORD the glory due unto his name: worship the LORD in the beauty of holiness. (2) KJV	John 14:27

For our Lord sits enthroned over the flood; the Lord is enthroned as King forever (v. 10).

Through all life's tempests, upheaval, fury, and storms, "The Lord gives strength to His people, the Lord blesses His people with peace" (v. 11).

Father, through these recent storms, the unexpected deaths of two family members; one tragic and traumatic and in a life way too young; both left tremendous holes causing great upheaval in the lives left behind, yet over all this tearing and tumult and more besides, You sit enthroned. You yet give strength to Your people, You yet bless Your people with peace. That peace is noticed. It is not explained. It is not rational, for it is not the world's peace. The world cannot understand it. In fact, neither can I; nevertheless, peace.

I treasure these words in the prologue of a much-loved book, *In This House of Breede* by Rumer Godden:

The motto was "Pax," but the word was set in a circle of thorns. Pax: peace, but what a strange peace, made of unremitting toil and effort, seldom with seen result; subject to constant interruptions, unexpected demands, short sleep at nights, little *comfort, sometimes scant food; beset with disappointments and usually misunderstood; yet peace all the same, undeviating, filled with joy and gratitude and love. "It is my own peace I give unto you."	Not notice, the world's peace.* (Godden, 1964)

Prayer:
Father, may we all, as we behold You high and lifted up in Your temple, simply cry, "Glory!" Thank You that we can come before You dressed in the beautiful robes of righteousness of Jesus Christ and thus worship You in the splendor of holiness. Father, it is both through the storms of life and through Your gracious presence filling our ordinary days that You transform us from one shade of glory to the next. Thank You for Your gift of peace gracing all our days.

Psalm 30: Joy in Hard Times

Focus Verse:	New Testament Verse:
You turned my wailing into dancing; you removed my sackcloth and clothed me with joy, (11)	I have told you this so that my joy may be in you and that your joy may be complete. John 15:11

For You:
- ❖ Lifted me out of the depths
- ❖ Did not let my enemies gloat over me
- ❖ Healed me
- ❖ Brought me up from the grave
- ❖ Spared me from going down into the pit

Hard times are hard! It is so hard to go through hard times when it seems God is hiding and not listening, and to remember to trust as we did during the times of security, prosperity, and apparent wellbeing. Yet, when looking back, it is the times of ease that turn out to be the most challenging times to maintain a right relationship with God, as there can be a tendency to begin relying on ourselves, forgetting our need for God. If we are not watchful, our *egos* begin to expand and gradually, bit by bit, Edge God Out.

Prayer:
Father, thank You for walking with us through all the seasons of life. Thank You that Your anger is momentary, but Your favor lasts a lifetime. Thank You that we can know with certainty that our nights of weeping will gradually brighten to mornings of rejoicing. Yet through it all, a steadfast presence, a strange peace, a complete joy

remains. You are not hiding; You do yet hear. Whether dark night or bright morning, my heart need never stop singing Your praises!

Psalm 31: Just What is Needed

Focus Verse:	New Testament Verse:
In the shelter of your presence, you hide them from the intrigues of men; in your dwelling place you keep them safe from accusing tongues (20)	Now to Him who is able to do immeasurably more than all we ask or imagine, according to his power that is at work within us, to him be glory in the church and in Christ Jesus through all generations, for ever and ever! Amen.
	Ephesians 3:20, 21

How wonderfully David, here, interweaves his pleading petitions with a recitation of God's promises.
The petitions:

- ❖ Let me never be put to shame; deliver me in Your righteousness (v. 1).
- ❖ Turn your ear to me, come quickly to my rescue; be my rock of refuge, a strong fortress to save me (v. 2).
- ❖ For the sake of Your name, lead and guide me (v. 3).
- ❖ Free me from the trap that is set for me (v. 4).
- ❖ Into Your hands I commit my spirit; redeem me (v. 5).
- ❖ Be merciful to me, O Lord, for I am in distress; my eyes, my soul, my body, my life, my years, my strength, my bones grow weak, fail, and are consumed with sorrow, grief, and anguish (vv. 9-10).
- ❖ Deliver me from my enemies who hold me in contempt, who slander and terrorize me; who conspire and plot against me (vv. 11-15).
- ❖ Let Your face shine on me; save me because I have cried out to You (vv. 16-17).

- ❖ Let the wicked be put to shame, their lying lips silenced (vv. 18).

Undergirding promises:

God is:
- ❖ A refuge
- ❖ My Deliverer
- ❖ Righteous
- ❖ My Rescuer
- ❖ My Rock
- ❖ My Guide
- ❖ My Redeemer
- ❖ The Truth
- ❖ One who sees my affliction and the anguish of my soul, thus knowing just what I need
- ❖ Loving (protecting me from entrapment, instead setting my feet in a spacious place)
- ❖ Merciful
- ❖ Light
- ❖ Good
- ❖ The Avenger
- ❖ Shelter (hiding me safely in His dwelling, away from intrigue and accusing tongues)
- ❖ Preserver of the faithful

Prayer:

Father, as I take David's words as my own in this Psalm, I, like him, witness my petitions once again turn to praise as I see with fresh eyes how You perfectly become to us just what is needed at just the right time. How great is Your goodness, which You have stored up for those who fear You. For You are able to do immeasurably more than all we ask or imagine, according to Your power that is at work within us through Christ Jesus. My times are in Your hands.

Psalm 32: My Hiding Place

Focus Verse:	New Testament Verse:
You are my hiding place, you will protect me from trouble and surround me with songs of deliverance. (7)	Set your minds on things above, not on earthly things. For you died, and your life is now hidden with Christ in God.
	Colossians 3:2, 3

How beautiful this is.
Not matter the destruction, despair, defeat, or depression, even as one traverses the valley of the shadow of death, songs of deliverance surround the believer.
Returning to a misshaped life after the death of a loved one
    <Even so, Your songs of deliverance surround me>
Dealing with a depressed, angry, desperately confused family member day after day
    <Even so, Your songs of deliverance surround me>
Facing the aftermath of hurricanes, floods, and fires
    <Even so, Your songs of deliverance surround me>
Terrorized by senseless attacks, mass murders, bitter anger, and profound evil
    <Even so, Your songs of deliverance surround me>
Despairing over lukewarm churches, apathy, and lack of commitment
    <Even so, Your songs of deliverance surround me>

Prayer:
Teach me, Father, to go to You, my hiding place; to seek Your protection in all the storms of life; to tune my ears to hear Your songs of deliverance surrounding me; even in the dark, even now.

Psalm 33: Making Music

Focus Verse:	New Testament Verse:
Sing joyfully to the LORD, you righteous; it is fitting for the upright to praise Him. (1)	May the God of hope fill you with all joy and peace as you trust in him, so that you may overflow with hope by the power of the Holy Spirit. Romans 15:13

We praise Him and make music with instruments, singing, and shouts of joy.
Why:
- The Word of the Lord is right and true
- He is faithful in all He does
- He loves righteousness and justice
- The earth is full of His unfailing love
- He is the creator and sustainer of all things: the heavens, the starry host, the waters of the sea
- His plans and purposes (not persons or nations) stand firm forever through all generations
- Our Lord sees and considers all we do
- Our Lord delivers
- He is our help, our shield
- Our hope is not in vain.

It is enough and more. His blessings and provision are overflowing.

My prayer is as Paul wrote to the Romans.

Prayer:
May Your hope fill me to overflowing with all joy and peace as I trust in You.

Psalm 34: A Hope That Does Not Disappoint

Focus Verse:	New Testament Verse:
I will extol the LORD at all times, his praise will always be on my lips. (1)	And hope does not disappoint us, because God has poured out his love into our hearts by the Holy Spirit, whom he has given us. Romans 5:5

Do I continually, consistently, regardless of the circumstances:
- ❖ Extol the Lord
- ❖ Praise the Lord
- ❖ Boast in the Lord
- ❖ Glorify the Lord
- ❖ Exalt His name
- ❖ Seek the Lord
- ❖ Look to the Lord
- ❖ Call on the Lord
- ❖ Fear the Lord
- ❖ Savor the goodness of the Lord
- ❖ Take refuge in the Lord?

When I do:
- ❖ I encourage the afflicted
- ❖ God answers
- ❖ He delivers us from fear
- ❖ Our lives reflect His radiance
- ❖ We are saved from all our troubles
- ❖ We experience God's goodness
- ❖ We are blessed, lacking nothing
- ❖ We are kept from evil words and lies

- ❖ We seek peace and pursue it
- ❖ The Lord hears and delivers from all trouble
- ❖ The Lord is close to the brokenhearted and saves those who are crushed in spirit
- ❖ We are protected
- ❖ We are redeemed
- ❖ We will not be condemned

Prayer:
Father, thanks for so extravagantly and lavishly pouring out Your love into our hearts by the Holy Spirit, whom You have given us. The hope I have placed in You will never disappoint me.

Psalm 35: I Am Your Salvation

Focus Verse:	New Testament Verse:
Say to my soul, I am your salvation. (3b)	No, in all these things we are more than conquerors through him who loved us.
	Romans 8:37
	Remember those in prison as if you were their fellow prisoners, and those who are mistreated as if you yourselves were suffering.
	Hebrews 13:3

This psalm is a prayer for the persecuted, those pushed beyond the limits of endurance who have made tremendous sacrifices and who seek assurance from their God that He will yet deliver:

- ❖ Those who have lost their livelihood for standing for their faith
- ❖ Those estranged from family and imprisoned for their belief in Christ
- ❖ The families of those shot, beheaded, or crucified for not forsaking their Lord
- ❖ Those ostracized and exiled from their tribes and communities for placing their faith in Jesus
- ❖ Those expelled from school because of their stand for their Savior

Prayer:
May each one clearly experience Your presence, protection, and provision. May each hear You say to them personally in their jail cell, the strange land they find themselves

in, their lonely habitation, their place of deep financial, emotional, and spiritual need: "I am your salvation." May each one fully recognize that in spite of seeming defeat, because of Your work through their lives, each one is indeed *more than a conqueror*... for neither death nor life, neither angels nor demons, neither the present nor the future, nor any powers, neither height nor depth, nor anything else in all creation, will be able to separate us from Your love that is in Christ Jesus (Rom. 8:27-29)

_____

_____

_____

_____

_____

_____

_____

_____

Psalm 36: Keeping Our Head in All Situations

Focus Verse:	New Testament Verse:
Your love, O LORD, reaches to the heavens, your faithfulness to the skies. Your righteousness is like the mighty mountains, your justice like the great deep. (5, 6)	Whoever has the Son has life; he who does not have the Son of God does not have life. 1 John 5:12

David's heart is heavy concerning the sinfulness of the wicked all around him.

His God of infinite love and faithfulness, His righteousness like the mighty mountains, and His justice like the great deep, is discounted in the minds and lives of the wicked who selfishly pursue their evil plots and sinful course. In their self-flattery they are unable to detect their sin. They do not reject what is wrong because they have reached the point of being unable. They have ceased to be wise and to do good. It is as if they have become blinded to the beauty and majesty of the Lord.

Paul warned his young protégé, Timothy, about this in his second letter to him:

Preach the Word; be prepared in season and out of season; correct, rebuke and encourage–with great patience and careful instruction. For the time will come when men will not put up with sound doctrine. Instead, to suit their own desires, they will gather around them a great number of teachers to say what their itching ears want to hear. They will turn their ears away from the truth and turn aside to myths. (2 Timothy 4:2-5)

How well David's deep concerns and Paul's warning resonate today. If anything, even more so. How apt, Paul's instructions that followed, "But you, keep your head in all situations" (v. 5).

Prayer:
Oh Father, do not let the proud, the wicked, the evildoers drive me away from You. Help me keep my head in all situations. Renew my mind, protect my thoughts, clarify my thinking. Protect and sustain me, oh Lord. Continue Your love to those who know You; Your righteousness to the upright in heart. Help us to always be prepared to share Your Word, Your Truth, with great patience and careful instruction. Through Your Son, Jesus Christ, we have been given the great privilege of knowing You. You, the Most High.

Now this is eternal life, that they may know you the only true God, and Jesus Christ, whom you have sent. (John 17:3)

Thank You for the gift of eternal life through the Son.

Psalm 37: Fret-free

Focus Verse:	New Testament Verse:
Do not fret because of evil men or be envious of those who do wrong; (1a)	Do not be overcome with evil but overcome evil with good. Romans 12:21

Instead of fretting or being envious of evil people:
- ❖ Trust in the Lord
- ❖ Do good
- ❖ Enjoy safe pasture
- ❖ Delight in the Lord
- ❖ Commit your way to Him
- ❖ Be still before the Lord and wait patiently for Him
- ❖ Refrain from anger and run from wrath
- ❖ Turn from evil and do good
- ❖ Be generous and lend freely
- ❖ Keep His way.

The trusting ones will:
- ❖ Dwell in the land and enjoy safe pasture
- ❖ Receive the desires of their hearts
- ❖ See their righteousness shine like the dawn; the justice of their cause like the noon day sun
- ❖ Inherit the land
- ❖ Enjoy great peace
- ❖ Be held up by the Lord
- ❖ Enjoy plenty
- ❖ Have an inheritance that endures forever
- ❖ Walk with a firm step
- ❖ Be upheld
- ❖ Dwell in the land forever.

How powerful and encouraging this is. Believers so vitally need it today, including me.

Prayer:
Father, help me not to be overcome with evil, but instead, overcome evil with good.

Psalm 38 (Penitential Psalm): Dealing with Guilt

Focus Verse:	New Testament Verse:
Come quickly to help me, O LORD my Savior. (22)	If we confess our sins, he is faithful and just and will forgive us our sins and purify us from all unrighteousness. 1 John 1:9

David, here, is in profound physical agony and deep mental anguish because of his own sin. His guilt is overwhelming him, the burden too heavy to bear. Nevertheless, in his realization of this, David cries out to his Jehovah God (v. 1); his sovereign Lord (Adonai) (v. 9); his God, Elohim (v. 15); his deliver, Jehovah, the One full of grace. Only a man after God's own heart, with a deep and intimate knowledge of his God, could experience such suffering because of his sinfulness. David could not bear to be separated from the Lover of his soul and thus pleads for God to not forsake him, to not be far away, but to "come quickly to help me, O Lord, my Savior." He fully owns up to and confesses his iniquity. No doubt partly what is so hard about the situation is that his sin (whatever it was) had damaged his testimony among his enemies waiting in the wings, ready to pounce on his slightest misstep.

What a lesson for believers today. Inevitably, we will make missteps. We will fall short. We will fail. But how beautiful it is that our loving Lord is eagerly waiting to come quickly and help. Our Lord and Savior specializes in bringing good from these situations of our own making. I am moved by David's suffering. Am I as disturbed by my sinfulness as he was about his own? Do I take sin seriously? Do I realize how damaging it is to my relationship with God, and how it blocks our communication and His ability to work in and through my life?

Prayer:
Father, thank You, that through Jesus, You have provided a way so that if we confess our sins, You are faithful and just and will forgive us of our sins and cleanse us from all unrighteousness. Make me quick to recognize and confess my sins. I want to hate sin as much as You do.

_____
_____
_____
_____
_____
_____
_____
_____

Psalm 39: Fixing Our Eyes on the Unseen

Focus Verse:	New Testament Verse:
... let me know how fleeting is my life (4)	So we fix our eyes not on what is seen, but on what is unseen. For what is seen is temporary, but what is unseen is eternal.
	2 Corinthians 4:18
	We live by faith, not by sight.
	2 Corinthians 5:7

This Psalm was written by David for Jeduthun, a harpist and leader of harpists, a member of the Levites.

If we rightly understand the brevity of our earthly lives against the backdrop of eternity, how would we live each of our few short days differently? Are we living self-centered or God-centered lives? What consumes our time, our energy, our resources, our talents, our time? How easy it is to become preoccupied with our wealth, our position, our accomplishments, until it soon becomes "all about me" and we find we have edged God out, allowing the world to gradually squeeze us into its mold. We find that we have become comfortable with being comfortable and along the way lost our sense of urgency about the whiteness of the harvest and being about our Father's business. We begin to focus on the seen instead of the unseen, thus begin to live by sight and not by faith.

Jonathon Edwards says it best: *"Lord, stamp eternity on my eyeballs."*

God is the highest good of the reasonable creature. The enjoyment of him is our proper; and is the only happiness with which our souls can be satisfied. To go to heaven, fully to enjoy God, is infinitely better than the most pleasant accommodations here. Better than fathers and mothers, husbands, wives, or children, or the company of any, or all earthly friends. These are but shadows; but the enjoyment of God is the substance. These are but scattered beams; but God is the sun. These are but streams; but God is the fountain. These are but drops, but God is the ocean. (Edwards, n.d.)
Jonathan Edwards, *The Works of Jonathan Edwards*, Vol. 17: Sermons and Discourses, 1730-1733

Prayer:
Father, may I daily honor You in my attitude, thoughts, ways; with my tongue, mouth, viewpoint; my perspective, activities; and the works of my hands, the places I go. May I look though my earthly daily circumstances directly to You. May my hope be only in You, my eyes focused on the unseen.

Psalm 40: Waiting... Patiently

Focus Verse:	New Testament Verse:
I waited patiently for the LORD; he turned to me and heard my cry. (1)	And we know that in all things God works for the good of those who love him, who have been called according to his purpose. Romans 8:28

David waited patiently for His Lord in a slimy pit in the mud and mire.
- ❖ Troubles without number surrounded him
- ❖ His sins (more than the hairs of his head) overtook him and blinded him
- ❖ His heart failed within him
- ❖ He was poor and needy.

Yet, at just the right time, David's Lord, **upon whom he patiently waited**, lifted David from the mud and mire and placed him on a firm rock. He gave David a new song, a hymn of praise to sing and proclaim.
The result: *Many will see and fear and put their trust in the Lord (v. 3).*

This, then, is the purpose in the suffering.
At just the right time, blessing upon blessing is bestowed on the one who makes the Lord his trust, does not look to the proud, and does not turn aside to false gods (v. 4). Many are the wonders God has planned for them (v. 5).

Prayer:

Father, thank You that we can know that in all things You work for the good of those who love You, who have been called according to Your purpose. I pray I will be faithful to You, especially through my suffering, so that many will see and fear and put their trust in You.

Janice Stauffer MacLeod

Psalm 41: Heavenward

Focus Verse:	New Testament Verse:
Praise be to the LORD, the God of Israel, from everlasting to everlasting. Amen and Amen. (13)	I press on toward the goal to win the prize for which God has called me heavenward in Christ Jesus.
	Philippians 3:14

With these fitting words, Book I-the Genesis section, of the five books of Psalms-ends.

Despite troubles, foes, sickness, malice, false accusations, and rumors, David, the song writer, trusts in his Lord's deliverance, protection, preservation, blessing, sustainment, restoration, and mercy and thus can declare, "Praise be to the Lord, the God of Israel, from everlasting to everlasting. Amen and Amen."

"I am the Alpha and Omega, The beginning and the end. The First and the Last" (Rev.1:18). From infinity past to infinity future, our great, gracious, most holy Jehovah remains in the last days revealed to us through His Son Jesus Christ-who is, who was, and who is to come-the Almighty.

During the most deep and desperate trials man sojourns through on earth, these truths yet remain. All must be seen against the backdrop of eternity. And thus we continue to "look up" and "turn heavenward."

Prayer:
Father, help me keep myself in God's love as I wait for the mercy of our Lord Jesus Christ to bring me to eternal life (Jude 21).

Help me press on heavenward.

Psalm 42: Remembering

Focus Verse:	New Testament Verse:
My soul is downcast within me; therefore I will remember you... (6)	Do not be anxious about anything, but in everything, by prayer and petition, with thanksgiving, present your requests to God. And the peace of God, which transcends all understanding, will guard your hearts and your minds in Christ Jesus.
	Philippians 4:6, 7

With this Psalm, Book II, the Exodus section begins.

"As the deer pants for streams of water, so my soul pants for You, O God. My soul thirsts for God, for the living God. When can I go and meet with God? My tears have been my food day and night, while men say to me all day long, 'Where is your God?'" (vv. 1-3)

This sorrowing psalmist is in the agonies of suffering so much so that he feels alienated from God's presence. And yet, this is a soul who has known true communion with his God. As he sinks into an almost desperate plea for His presence, his mind yet brings to remembrance those times of fellowship, provision, and deliverance. As he alternatively "looks up" and then is swept down again in waves of grief, he realizes his deliverance is in this remembering, holding fast to the rock-solid promises even in the darkest despair. And thus, *"my soul is downcast within me; therefore I will remember you."*

Remembering. Whether in the depths of the valley or on the peaks of the mountains. "From the land of the Jordan, the heights of Hermon–from Mount Mizar" (v. 6).

Remembering. Even as "deep calls to deep," realizing it is the roar of *Your* waterfalls, *Your* waves, *Your* breakers that have swept over me (v. 7).

Remembering. In the day and through the long watches of the night. "By day the Lord directs his love, at night his song is with me–a prayer to the God of my life" (v. 8). Knowing who God is, knowing His Word and His character, and simply standing on His promises regardless of emotions or circumstances will ultimately lead the way out of the darkness. Memorizing verses when crushing emotional pain threatens to topple our sanity is a way of steadying our thinking and filling our minds with truths from God's Word, providing a strong foundation for gaining our footing.

Prayer:
O Father, my soul is downcast within me; therefore I will remember You...

_____
_____
_____
_____
_____
_____
_____
_____

Psalm 43: Light and Truth

Focus Verse:	New Testament Verse:
Send forth your light and your truth, let them guide me; let them bring me to your holy mountain, to the place where you dwell. (3)	I want to know Christ and the power of his resurrection and the fellowship of sharing in his sufferings, becoming like him in his death, and so, somehow, to attain to the resurrection from the dead.
	Philippians 3:10, 11

Indeed, believers should challenge themselves as the sorrowing psalmist from Psalm 42 does as he continues his prayer here: "Why must I go about mourning, oppressed by the enemy?" (v. 2)

And again, repeated from the previous prayer, "Why are you downcast, O my soul? Why so disturbed within me?" (v. 5)

Instead, put your hope in God, your Savior.

❖ His light
❖ His truth
❖ His guidance...

will safely pilot His own to the very dwelling place of God-our true home.

"Then will I go to the altar of God, to God, my joy and my delight" (v. 4).

Always, Father, the altar. The *acceptance with joy*. The laying down of myself, my will, my selfish desires. The relinquishment. The way to Your presence is always first through the altar.

For, I want to know Christ and the power of His resurrection, and the fellowship of sharing in His sufferings, becoming like

Him in His death, and so somehow, to attain to the resurrection from the dead (Phil. 3:10-11).

Prayer:
Remind me, Father, to remember.

Psalm 44: Inseparable

Focus Verse:	New Testament Verse:
All this happened to us, though we had not forgotten you or been false to your covenant. (17)	For I am convinced that neither death nor life, neither angels nor demons, neither the present nor the future, nor any powers, neither height nor depth, nor anything else in all creation, will be able to separate us from the love of God that is in Christ Jesus our Lord. Romans 8:38

What was the "this" that happened to the subjects of this Psalm? They were:
- Rejected
- Forced to retreat
- Plundered
- Devoured
- Scattered
- Sold for a pittance
- Made a reproach, an object of scorn and derision, a byword
- Disgraced, taunted, reproached, and reviled

Bad things do happen to good people (people redeemed, bought for the price of the blood of Jesus, who remain true to their Lord and Savior).

A husband, the father of fifteen children, many adopted, and youngest son of a family of five children that had already lost the eldest to cancer, was suddenly killed in a terrible accident, leaving a gaping hole in his family. Hurricanes, fires, tornadoes, wars, mass shootings, acts of terrorism and hatred and evil affect both the redeemed and those who reject You alike.

Yet, through all this seemingly meaningless suffering, we find Your love perseveres. "For I am convinced" writes the apostle Paul to the Roman believers, "that neither death nor life, neither angels nor demons, neither the present not the future, nor any powers, neither height nor depth, nor anything else in all creation will be able to separate us from the love of God that is in Christ Jesus our Lord" (Rom. 8:37).

Corrie ten Boom and her sister, Betsi experienced the depths of this love while suffering in the horrific Ravensbruk concentration camp during World War II, realizing even as their observable external life grew every day more horrible, the other life they lived with God grew daily better and better, truth upon truth, glory upon glory. Even as she lay dying in a filthy hospital, Betsi urged her sister, "We must tell people what we have learned here. We must tell them that there is no pit so deep that He is not deeper still" (Boom, 1971).

Indeed, after her miraculous release, Corrie ten Boom committed the rest of her life to be a "tramp for the Lord" to share this message of God's amazing love to people around the globe, including even her former prison guard.

Prayer:
Father, thank You, that absolutely nothing, now nor ever, will be able to separate me from Your love. Help me share Your love with others today, especially those in deep pits of suffering.

Psalm 45 (a Messianic Psalm): The Mystery

Focus Verse:	New Testament Verse:
My heart is stirred by a noble theme as I recite my verses for the king; my tongue is the pen of a skillful writer. (1)	Let us rejoice and be glad and give him glory! For the wedding of the Lamb has come, and his bride has made herself ready. Revelation 19:7

In this Messianic Psalm, this royal wedding song, our Savior, King, and Lord is praised as:
- Most excellent
- Anointed with grace
- Eternally beloved
- Mighty
- Splendid
- Majestic
- Victorious on behalf of truth, humility, and righteousness
- Displaying awesome deeds
- A conqueror
- Everlasting
- Ruling with justice
- Set above all others
- Completely righteous
- Anointed with joy
- Dressed in fragrant robes
- Dwelling in adorned palaces
- Enjoying the music of strings

You, our Christ and Lord, will receive Your beloved and beautiful bride, Your church.

"In reading this, then," Paul writes to the Ephesians, *"you will be able to understand my insight into the mystery of Christ, which was not made known to men in other generation as it has now been revealed by the Spirit to God's holy apostles and prophets"* (Eph. 3:4-5).

Great is the mystery of godliness.

Prayer:
Prepare me, prepare us, to be Your royal bride.

Psalm 46: Eyewitnesses of His Majesty

Focus Verse:	New Testament Verse:
God is our refuge and strength, an ever-present help in trouble. (1)	"but we were eyewitnesses of his majesty." 2 Peter 1:16b

This is the first of a Psalms trilogy (46, 47, 48).

Oh, that we would be still and know that He is God. That we would recognize-regardless of our rebellion, foolishness, or stubbornness-God will be exalted among the nations, God will be exalted in the earth (v. 10). He is ever-present.

It is in this being still:
- This settling down of chaotic cluttered thinking
- This tuning in of distracted ears
- This refocusing of our spiritual eyes so "the things on earth grow strangely dim in the light of His glory and grace"

It is then that we come to appreciate His ever-presence, even in the midst of our troubles, and thus can declare as the psalmist did that we will not fear though the most catastrophic thing we can imagine:
- The earth gives way and the mountains fall into the heart of the sea (v. 2)
- Waters roar and foam and mountains quake with their surging (. v3)
- Nations are in uproar and kingdoms fall; the earth melts (v. 6)

For the Lord Almighty is with us, the God of Jacob is our fortress (v. 7). He is ever-present.

Prayer:
Father, this day, help me see through all the darkness, wickedness, upheaval, chaos, and confusion, to see (be an eyewitness to) Your ever-present majesty.

_____
_____
_____
_____
_____
_____
_____
_____

Psalm 47: Thy Kingdom Come-Today

Focus Verse:	New Testament Verse:
For God is the King of all the earth; sing to him a psalm of praise. (7)	and there before me was a throne in heaven with someone sitting on it. Revelation 4:2b

The second of this Psalms trilogy (46, 47, 48) recognizes our exalted God as not just King of His own people, but, in fact, of the *entire earth*:

❖ *Every* nation
❖ *Every* person
❖ *All* nobles and kings

Thus, Jesus taught us to pray, "Our Father who art in heaven, hallowed by Thy Name, Thy kingdom come, Thy will be done *on Earth* [even now] as it is in heaven." (Matthew 6:9, 10)

For *today* (right now and forever):

❖ Our God reigns over the nations
❖ Our God is seated on His holy throne
❖ Our God is highly exalted.

We-as His people, His inheritance, the people of Jacob, the people of the God of Abraham-should thus live victoriously, celebrate with clapping of hands, singing of praises, and shouting cries of joy. How awesome is the Lord most high, the great King over all the earth!

Prayer:
Father, thank You that in heaven, there is a throne. Thank You that someone is sitting on that throne. How I look forward to joining that huge heavenly choir in triumphantly singing Your praises, for You are worthy, our Lord and

God, to receive glory and honor and power. Until then, work through me that Your kingdom may come, Your will be done on Earth *even today* as it is in heaven.

Psalm 48: Guarding What Has Been Entrusted

Focus Verse:	New Testament Verse:
Walk about Zion, go around her, count her towers, consider all her ramparts, view her citadels, that you may tell of them to the next generation. (12, 13)	Timothy, guard what has been entrusted to your care. 1 Timothy 6:20a

This, the third of the Psalms trilogy (46, 47, 48), expresses the praise expressed by one, who, having faced deadly peril, has experienced a great deliverance through the powerful right hand of his God. There is expressed a profound realization and assurance that "this God is our God for ever and ever; He will be our guide even to the end." This is a God whose powerful right hand is filled with righteousness.

Thus the significance, the weight of responsibility of the verse selected-how critical it is that we thoroughly examine and understand the amazing nature of our God, His Word, and His perfect plan and provision for His people, that we might tell of them to the next generation.

❖ Count her towers
❖ Consider well her ramparts (protective barrier; a bulwark)
❖ View her citadels (a fortress that commands a city)

Prayer:
Father, help me to daily share my story of redemption, to carefully recount the miracle that You have worked in my own life, the way You continue to perform Your transforming work in my life, and how You stand at my

side and give me strength, protection, and security. Help me safely guard what has been entrusted to me. The next generation needs to hear my story.

_____
_____
_____
_____
_____
_____
_____
_____

Psalm 49: The Backdrop of Eternity

Focus Verse:	New Testament Verse:
But God will redeem my life from the grave. he will surely take me to himself. (15)	Since, then, you have been raised with Christ, set your hearts on things above, where Christ is seated at the right hand of God. Set your minds on thing above, not on earthly things. For you died, and your life is now hidden with Christ in God. When Christ, who is your life appears, you also will appear with him in glory.
	Colossians 3:1-4

This song has application to all people, both:
- ❖ Low and high
- ❖ Rich and poor
- ❖ Wise and foolish

It is a song from a psalmist, a songwriter, who is beginning to see the temporal world around him against the backdrop of eternity. He shares a truth, for him recently grasped, that no man-no matter how cunning, wealthy, deceitful, or wicked-can ever buy his way out of avoiding not just physical but spiritual death. No payment will ever be enough. This side of the cross we understand that only the sacrificial blood of Jesus Christ can redeem a soul from death. Indeed, a man who has riches without understanding, is like the beasts that perish (all his sophistication and splendor will not descend to the grave with him). Thus Jesus taught His disciples: *Do not store up for yourselves treasures on earth where moth and rust destroy, and where thieves break in and steal. But store up for yourselves treasures in heaven... for where your treasure is, there you heart will be also* (Matthew 6:19, 21).

Janice Stauffer MacLeod

Prayer:

Father, thank You that not only will You redeem my soul from the grave, You will also take me to Yourself. In response to this, instead of focusing on earthly things, I want to daily seek You first, setting my heart on things above, where Christ is seated at Your right hand. Help me come to understand that I have died, that my life is now hidden with Christ in You. It is because of this that I will live for eternity in Your presence.

_____
_____
_____
_____
_____
_____
_____
_____

Psalm 50: The Sacrifice of Praise

Focus Verse:	New Testament Verse:
He who sacrifices thank offerings honors me, and he prepares the way so that I may show him the salvation of God. (23)	Therefore, I urge you, brothers, in view of God's mercy, to offer your bodies as living sacrifices, holy and pleasing to God — this is your spiritual act of worship.
Whoso offereth praise glorifieth me: and to him that ordereth his conversation aright will I shew the salvation of God. (23) (KJV)	Romans 12:1

Our mighty God, Lord of lords, full of grace and glory, beauty, and light:
- ❖ Speaks
- ❖ Summons
- ❖ Rebukes those who forget God

And it is the one who sacrifices, not in hypocritical worship, but in true gratitude and praise, that beautifully prepares the way for God's salvation to be fully revealed. It is this constancy, steadfastness, this clinging and refusing to let go, regardless of all temporal circumstances; this leaving all on the altar, dying to self, that opens the way that You in all Your beauty may shine forth in our lives. The selected verse was such a gift, a treasured teaching in a time of great need. This consistent honoring of God and speaking up for Him and not failing to say things in our daily conversation that would honor him, thus "Thy Kingdom come, Thy will be done on earth as it is in heaven." Watchman Nee says it well: "Therefore every believer can stand for God and for his will in the place where he lives and works. He can occupy that piece of territory and hold it for God" (Nee, n.d.). For wherever the believer walks is holy ground.

Prayer:
Father, I offer to You myself, daily, on the altar. My mind, please renew it. My ears, please waken me, Lord, to listen like one being taught so I can hear Your still, small voice, teaching me the words of healing that will sustain the weary. My eyes, open my eyes that I may behold wondrous things from Your Word; that I may increasingly focus not on what is seen, but on what is unseen. My heart, cleanse it from all selfishness that Your love may be poured in, abundantly, overflowing into the lives of those around me. My hands, make them Yours. May I serve others in Your name. My feet, make them swift and beautiful for You, fitted with the readiness that comes from the gospel of peace.

_____
_____
_____
_____
_____
_____
_____
_____

Psalm 51: A Clean Heart

Focus Verse: Create in me a clear heart, O God, and renew a steadfast spirit in me. (10)	New Testament Verse:
	If we confess our sins, he is faithful and just and will forgive us our sins and purify us from all unrighteousness.
	1 John 1:9
	For God is greater than our hearts, and He knows everything.
	1 John 3:20

In this greatest and most well known of penitential psalms, David expresses the great agony his sin of adultery and murder has caused in separating him from fellowship with his God. It was not just the sin, but the sinner that needed dealing with. David pleaded for:

- ❖ Mercy
- ❖ Compassion
- ❖ Unfailing love
- ❖ The blotting out of his transgression
- ❖ Washing away of all his iniquity
- ❖ Cleansing
- ❖ Truth in the inner parts
- ❖ Wisdom in the innermost place
- ❖ Joy and gladness
- ❖ The creation of a pure heart and a steadfast spirt
- ❖ The right to once again be in God's presence and to have His Holy Spirit with him
- ❖ Restoration of his relationship and fellowship with God
- ❖ A willing spirit to sustain him
- ❖ The right and ability to teach others through the example of a God who saves, forgives, and cleanses

- ❖ His lips to be opened to declare God's praise
- ❖ The prospering of Zion so there would be righteous sacrifices to offer

David's pleas reveal the depth of his relationship with his God. He fully recognizes God does not look at the outer man, but at the innermost places of the heart. David deeply desires to be cleansed thoroughly, from the inside out. His prayer is a model prayer of confession for believers today.

Prayer:
Father, of all these requests of David, I most need and plead for steadfastness. Thank You that when we confess our sins, You are faithful and just and will forgive us our sins and cleanse us from all unrighteousness.

Psalm 52: Flourishing in Tough Times

Focus Verse:	New Testament Verse:
But I am like an olive tree flourishing in the house of God; I trust in God's unfailing love forever and ever. (8)	But the fruit of the Spirit is love, joy, peace, patience, kindness, goodness, faithfulness, gentleness and self-control. Galatians 5:22, 23

The flourishing is the result of deep roots in the Word of God. Well placed trust in His unfailing and enduring love resulting in fruit in season.

Against this, Doeg, the Edomite, in spite of his boasting, plotting, deceit, evil, and falsehood is laughable, easily uprooted, and ruined forever.

What Doegs of Edom am I facing?
- ❖ Arrogance and boasting
- ❖ Chaotic politics
- ❖ Anger and violence
- ❖ An unstable economy
- ❖ Endless deceit, lying
- ❖ Deluded thinking

Yet, I am like a flourishing olive tree, like a green tree planted by the rivers of water, yielding fruit in season.

Prayer:
Father, help me trust in You to keep me flourishing even in a sun-parched land, yielding just the right fruit at just the right time through Your indwelling.

Psalm 53: Willingly or Unwillingly

Focus Verse:	New Testament Verse:
There they were, overwhelmed with dread, where there was nothing to dread. (5)	At that time the sign of the Son of Man will appear in the sky, and all the nations of the earth will mourn. They will see the Son of Man coming in the clouds of the sky, with power and great glory. Matthew 24:30

This Psalm is also in Book 1, Psalm 14. But here, in Book 2, the name for God is Elohim instead of Jehovah. This has been the case throughout Book 2. Here, an extra phrase is added to verse 5: *There they were, overwhelmed with dread, where there was nothing to dread.*

There are Bible stories where this has happened, including during King Hezekiah's reign and the sudden and unexpected departure and annihilation of Sennacherib's army (Isa. 37). This is the occasion when Hezekiah, having received a threatening letter from Sennacherib's messengers, immediately took it the temple of the Lord and spread it out before the Lord. This was his prayer, and it is a good one to commit to memory to repeat in our own desperate circumstances, filling in with our own situation:

O Lord Almighty, God of Israel, enthroned between the cherubim, You alone are God over all the kingdoms of the earth. You have made heaven and earth. Give ear, O Lord, and hear; open Your eyes, O Lord, and see, listen to all the words Sennacherib has sent to insult the living God... Now, O Lord our God, deliver us from his hand, so that all kingdoms on earth may know that You alone, O Lord are God. (Isaiah 37:14-20)

Men will fear God, willingly or ultimately unwillingly to their demise. God is powerful and mighty. He rules over all. He is the Creator and Sustainer of all things.

At that time the sign of the Son of Man will appear in the sky and all the nations of the earth will mourn. They will see the Son of Man coming in the clouds of the sky, with power and great glory (Matt. 24:30).

Prayer:
Jesus, we yet wait Your return as our Lord and Savior, Jesus Christ, our Messiah, King.

Psalm 54: The Gift of Encouragement

Focus Verse:	New Testament Verse:
Save me, O God, by Your name; vindicate me by your might (1)	But encourage one another daily, as long as it is called Today, so that none of you may be hardened by sin's deceitfulness.
	Hebrews 3:13
	Let us not give up meeting together, as some are in the habit of doing, but let us encourage one another–and all the more as you see the Day approaching.
	Hebrews 10:25

David penned this Psalm when on the run from King Saul, when David was betrayed by the Ziphites, among whom he had hidden (1 Sam. 23). This is a remarkable story to read. It is interesting to try to imagine when exactly during this tumult that David paused to record these lines.

In 1 Sam. 23:16, we learn it was ahead of this betrayal that David's dear friend and King Saul's son, Jonathon, had come to David *"and helped him find strength in God."*

How beautiful this is. We cannot know, but it is possible that this time of encouragement might well have led to David's heart-felt plea to his God and his strong declaration of faith recorded here: *Surely God is my help; the Lord is the one who sustains me (v. 4). For He has delivered me from all my troubles and my eyes have looked in triumph on my foes (v. 7).*

How important it is that we, as fellow believers, take time to encourage, strengthen, and pray for one another. There may well be Davids, other persecuted believers, to whom we could be a Jonathon this very day. Our words of encouragement could be just the help needed by suffering believers to lead them to a renewal and strengthening of their faith.

Prayer:
Father, help me to be an encouragement to someone today. In Your name.

Psalm 55: Relinquishing

Focus Verse:	New Testament Verse:
Cast your cares on the LORD and He will sustain you; he will never let the righteous fall. (22)	But He said to me, "My grace is sufficient for you, for my power is made perfect in weakness." Therefore I will boast all the more gladly about my weaknesses, so that Christ's power may rest on me. 2 Corinthians 12:9

It is in this casting, this relinquishing, that we find strength: His strength made perfect.

In this particular instance (unknown), it is the malice, abuse, violence, strife, threats, lies, stares, anger, and revilement of David's enemies toward him that so troubled him and brought him suffering, anguish, terror, fear, trembling, horror, and an urge to flee. Worse, these insults were coming from someone who had been a companion, a close friend with whom David once enjoyed sweet fellowship.

It is this that leads David to call on his God continually, evening, morning, and noon, to cast his cares on the Lord. This burden is too much, too heavy. David is left staggering under its weight; his senses are spinning and he has lost his footing. It is in the casting of his cares on the Lord that David experiences the Lord's sufficient grace, the Lord's power made perfect in his weakness. Thus as Paul, years later, would experience, he could then delight in weakness, insults, hardships, persecutions, and difficulties; for in these darkest moments of human weakness, then is God's grace and strength fully realized.

Prayer:
Father, what a comfort these verses have been to me over the years. Thanks for Your grace, all sufficient. It is always enough and more.

Psalm 56: When I Am Afraid-I Will Not Be Afraid

Focus Verse:	New Testament Verse:
When I am afraid, I will trust in You. (3)	For God did not give us a spirit of timidity, but a spirit of power, of love and of self-discipline.
	2 Timothy 1:7

David had good reason to be afraid through all the years of fleeing Saul's relentless, hot, murderous pursuit (1 Sam. 23-31).

And yet, *When I am afraid, I will trust in you (v. 3). In God whose word I praise; in God I trust; I will not be afraid* (v. 4). *In God, whose word I praise, in the Lord, whose word I praise-In God I trust; I will not be afraid. What can man do to me?* (vv. 10-11).

David decides, even in the deepest darkness of his fears, to trust in his God. He repeatedly declares his trust in his God. The result: *When I am afraid-I will not be afraid.*

He places his hopes and his trust in his God's rock-solid Word. I can imagine David reciting scripture, singing scripture songs (even if silently to himself) as he alternatively fled and hid. For him, it was a decision. And so for us it is too. When I am afraid-I will not be afraid.

Prayer:
Father, with David, I praise You. For You have delivered me from death and my feet from stumbling, that I may walk before God in the light of life (v. 13). Father, I pray this prayer for all persecuted Christians everywhere. May Your Word richly comfort each one as they decide to trust

in You-to decide that when they are afraid to not be afraid. Father, thank You too, that our fears and tears matter to You so much that You keep a record of our laments and list our tears in Your scroll. How I love Your Word.

Psalm 57: Steadfastness

Focus Verse:	New Testament Verse:
My heart is steadfast, O God; my heart is steadfast; I will sing and make music. (7)	And the God of all grace, who called you to his eternal glory in Christ, after you have suffered a little while, will himself restore you and make you strong, firm and steadfast.
	1 Peter 5:10

David, who is fleeing King Saul, who is hotly pursuing him, determined to kill him, describes his situation. *I am in the midst of lions; I lie among ravenous beasts–men whose teeth are spears and arrows, whose tongues are sharp swords (v. 4). They spread a net for my feet. I was bowed down in distress. They dug a pit in my path (v. 6).*

It is in this setting that David sings, makes music, praises his God, exalts his God, entreats his God for His mercy, refuge, love, faithfulness, and protection.

This is the prophet Hosea declaring with total acceptance with joy, *"though the fig tree does not blossom..."*

It is Job steadfastly declaring, *"If He slays me, yet will I love Him."*

It is Paul and Silas, centuries later, singing praise to God in their jail cell.

This is the richest of human communion with the Almighty God.

Again, as in Psalm 55, here is relinquishment, the total casting of one's self on God, the total dying to self that God's power may fully be manifest. The acceptance with joy sort of total surrender.

Janice Stauffer MacLeod

Prayer:
Father, I borrow David's words for my prayer: my heart is steadfast, O God; my heart is steadfast; I will sing and make music.

Psalm 58 (an Imprecatory Psalm): Loving the Tough to Love

Focus Verse:	New Testament Verse:
Then men will say, "Surely the righteous still are rewarded; surely there is a God who judges the earth. (11)	"But love your enemies, do good to them, and lend to them without expecting to get anything back. Then your reward will be great, and you will be sons of the Most High, because he is kind to the ungrateful and wicked. Be merciful, just as your Father is merciful." Luke 6:35, 36

In this Psalm, David condemns unjust, corrupt, wicked, violent government and pleads with his God to hasten that day of ultimate judgment in which his God will completely, utterly, dramatically destroy all evil and reward the righteous.

How does a believer on this side of the cross respond to this? We must remember and recognize:

- ❖ Except for the blood of Jesus Christ cleansing me from all sin and replacing my filthy rags with the righteous robes of Jesus Christ, I too would deserve the treatment graphically described by David. Thank You, Jesus, for saving my soul.
- ❖ Jesus intentionally has kept us in the world even though as believers we are no longer of this word and travel as strangers here. Jesus specifically prayed for our protection from the evil one. We live in a world sinking deeper and deeper into the downward spiral of gross wickedness and evil; among people whom God has given over to the sinful desires of their

hearts. Even now the wrath of God is being revealed from heaven against all the ungodliness and wickedness of men who are suppressing the truth by their wickedness.

- ❖ Jesus taught us to pray for our enemies; to overcome evil with good, to leave room for God's wrath, and to leave it to God to avenge according to His perfect plan.
- ❖ Jesus ever stands before the throne of grace and intercedes for us. He has prepared us and will carry us through.

Prayer:
Father, thank You for Your perfect plan. For paying the price of my sin. For perfectly equipping me as I sojourn through this world.

Psalm 59: My Strength

Focus Verse:	New Testament Verse:
O my Strength, I watch for you; you, O God, are my fortress, my loving God. (9)	So then, just as you received Christ Jesus as Lord, continue to live in him, rooted and built up in him, strengthened in the faith as you were taught, and overflowing with thankfulness.
	Colossians 1:6, 7

The theme here: "The Lord is my strength (Defender)." Again, 2 Cor. 12:9-10: "His power made perfect in my weakness; His grace sufficient" comes to mind.

This Psalm was written early on in David's dealing with King Saul's increasingly irrational, "mad," evil spirit-led, violent behavior toward him. From those early days and all the way through, we see David's steadfast reliance on his God, trusting in his God to ultimately work in all things for his good.

Father, I want to learn to rely constantly and consistently on You as my strength. Teach me to rise above my circumstances to let Your strength fully operate through me. Focus my mind on You and Your strength.

Turn my eyes to watch for You to act on my behalf and for my good.

Still my heart so that I will be able to wait and let You go before me.

Even while false accusations, lies, and evil are swirling all about me, open my mouth to sing of Your strength and Your love, for You are my strength. In all these things, we are more than conquerors.

Prayer:
I worship You, oh Lord.

_____
_____
_____
_____
_____
_____
_____
_____

Psalm 60: Our Banner

Focus Verse:	New Testament Verse:
But for those who fear you, you have raised a banner to be unfurled against the bow. (4)	Finally, be strong in the Lord and in his mighty power. Ephesians 6:10

We first see the name "Jehovah Nissi" after the amazing battle of Israel at Rephidim, where victory was achieved as long as Moses, supported by Aaron and Hur, kept his arms raised while Joshua waged the battle. The altar Moses built after the victory was named Jehovah Nissi, "Jehovah our Banner" (Exod. 17).

David recognizes this truth: it is only through Jehovah Nissi that any battle is won. When we fail to lift our arms to God, we lose the battle and thus disgrace the banner, the very name of God, the banner of truth. It is only as we relinquish our lives, our struggles, and our battles to Him that He is able to work His power and strength perfectly through us and thus lead us to victory.

I am learning that in my own life, in regards to a particular struggle. In journeying though the past few Psalms, I have discovered the lesson I most need to learn is relinquishment: acceptance with joy.

There are broader lessons here too, for our nation and our abandonment of God as Jehovah Nissi, our Banner. There are clearly end-times applications when looking at cross references (Isa. 11:10, 12; 18:3), thus this Psalm can guide our prayers for our nation and for our world, as well as guide us in our own personal battles.

Prayer:

Father, might we rightly honor Your great name and wave Your banner high, that truth, Your truth might be victorious, even today, on earth as it is in heaven.

Psalm 61: From the End of My Rope

Focus Verse:	New Testament Verse:
From the ends of the earth I call to you, I call as my heart grows faint; lead me to the rock that is higher than I. (2)	But the Lord stood at my side and gave me strength, so that through me the message might be fully proclaimed and all the Gentiles might hear it. And I was delivered from the lion's mouth. 2 Timothy 4:17

David likely penned this Psalm while in exile from his beloved city, possibly during his son Absalom's rebellion. He may have considered the words from Deut. 4:29, the Law he would have known so well: *But if from there you seek the Lord your God, you will find him if you look for him with all of your heart and with all of your soul.*

David was in agony of spirit, deep suffering, possibly even realizing his own actions and decisions had led to his current situation and thus it is, that this man after God's heart turned again to the *"rock that is higher than I."* knowing that regardless of his location or circumstances, his God would surely come to his aid.

What a wonderful prayer for every wayward Christian living a life of shame and regret, in paraphrase:

Prayer:
From the end of my rope, I call to you.

Psalm 62: This I Know

Focus Verse:	New Testament Verse:
One thing God has spoken, two things have I heard: that you, O God, are strong, and that you, O LORD are loving. (11, 12a)	I can do everything through him who gives me strength. Philippians 4:13

Here, David builds on the idea of God as "the rock that is higher than I." It is God and God alone who:
- ❖ Provides rest for the soul
- ❖ Delivers salvation
- ❖ Is my fortress, my refuge, my hope
- ❖ Can be trusted at all times.

David has learned two rock-solid truths about his God that are etched in his mind and heart. Even as his world is shaken and enemies surround him, David grasps these truths as an anchor:
- ❖ You, O Lord, are strong
- ❖ You, O Lord are loving

It is enough. I once rediscovered this verse on the very morning of the day that I later, unexpectedly, found I had lost my job in a series of layoffs. Immediately, these words read earlier in the morning filled my mind, my soul, my very being with peace. Regardless, my Lord is strong. My Lord is loving. All else fades in comparison.

Prayer:
Father, thank You that when I am overwhelmed, You lead me to the rock that is higher than I. At all times and all circumstances, Your strength and unfailing love are available to me.

Psalm 63: The Power to Grasp

Focus Verse:	New Testament Verse:
My soul clings to You; your right hand upholds me. (8)	I pray that out of his glorious riches he may strengthen you with power through his Spirit in your inner being, so that Christ may dwell in your hearts through faith. And I pray that you, being rooted and established in love, **may have power,** together with all the saints, **to grasp** how wide and long and high and deep is the love of Christ, and to know this love that surpasses knowledge–that you may be filled to the measure of all the fullness of God. Ephesians 3:16-19

It is in the deserts of life, in the dry and weary land where there is no water, that a soul becomes an earnest seeker, thirsty and longing for the renewed presence of the God remembered and once beheld in all His power, glory, and love. It is God, and God alone, the desperate soul, stripped of all else, comes to realize, that will satisfy. Thus, the clinging at all costs, as did Jacob, wrestling with God, declaring, "I will not let you go until you bless me."

While it is true there is nothing left to do in these situations but cling, it is yet a choice, a determination to cling. Then the beautiful revelation that the God so desperately sought is near and is in fact upholding the grasping seeker with His right hand, thus making the desire to cling and the power to grasp even possible.

Prayer:

Father, how often I have pondered and puzzled over this clinging, this grasping. How treasured and often repeated are these words of Jacob in my own times of quiet desperation. Yet now, You layer in this deeper truth so that I can now declare with a more profound understanding, "I will not let You go until You bless me, because You will never let me go."

_____
_____
_____
_____
_____
_____
_____
_____

Psalm 64: Being Afraid of Being Afraid

Focus Verse:	New Testament Verse:
Hear my voice, O God, in my prayer: preserve my life from fear of the enemy. (1) (KJV)	Therefore put on the full armor of God, so that when the day of evil comes, you may be able to stand your ground, and after you have done everything, to stand. Ephesians 6:13

This petition of David is shared in the King James Version. A gleaming truth and a vital prayer for every believer every day: "preserve my life from fear of the enemy." G. Campbell Morgan relates the experiences of the soldiers during the "Great War," as he refers to World War I. The soldiers consistently related that their greatest fear was that they should be filled with fear. Being afraid of being afraid becomes thus the very impetus of their courage (Morgan, 1994).

This Psalm builds on the gleaming truth revealed in the previous Psalm. My very ability to not fear, to cling (the power to grasp) is only possible through the upholding right hand of the God so earnestly sought, and thus the need for every believer every day to pray David's petition, "preserve my life from fear of the enemy."

We pray this when we pray the Lord's Prayer: "and lead us not into temptation, but deliver us from evil." It is spending time in our all-powerful God's presence, rightly arming ourselves, that equips us to take our stand and to not give in to fear.

Prayer:
Hear my voice, O God, in my prayer: preserve my life from fear of the enemy.

Psalm 65: The Ends of the Earth

Focus Verse:	New Testament Verse:
You answer us with awesome deeds of righteousness, O God our Savior, the hope of all the ends of the earth and of the farthest seas, (5)	pray continually; 1 Thessalonians 5:17

In this Psalm of first waiting in God's presence-of praise, confession, petition, thanksgiving, worship, and joy-the psalmist, David, recognized anew that it is God alone who:

- ❖ Hears prayer
- ❖ Forgives the transgressions of all who will come to Him
- ❖ Fills us with good things
- ❖ In answer to our petition works His awesome deeds of righteousness (the perfect provision, the perfect plan)
- ❖ Is the hope of all the ends of the earth.

How wonderful to know that in response to my prayer, my God, my Savior, will without fail work His awesome deeds of righteousness. The right answer at the right time in the right way. This is true for all my fellow believers in every corner of the globe, no matter the circumstances. Thus we unite in our universal prayer:

Prayer:
Our Father who art in heaven, hallowed be Thy name. Thy kingdom come, Thy will be done on Earth as it is in heaven...

Psalm 66: Come and See

Focus Verse:	New Testament Verse:
Come and see what the LORD [God] has done; how awesome his work in man's behalf! (5)	That which was from the beginning, which we have heard, which we have seen with our eyes, which we have looked at and our hands have touched–this we proclaim concerning the Word of life.
	1 John 1:1

The shepherds, upon hearing the angels' message, said to one another, "Let us go to Bethlehem and *see* this thing that has happened, which the Lord has told us about" (Luke 2:15).

Simeon, upon *seeing* the child Jesus when His parents presented Him in the temple declared, "My eyes have *seen* Your salvation which You have prepared in the sight of all people" (Luke 2:30-31).

The Magi, when they *saw* the star, were overjoyed. On coming to the house, they *saw* the child with His mother, Mary, and they bowed down and worshiped Him (Matt. 2:10-11).

"Come and *see*," Phillip said as he invited Nathaniel to meet Jesus (John 1:46).

The blind beggar who called out for Jesus when He was passing by, when Jesus asked, "What do you want Me to do for you?" answered, "Lord, I want to *see*." He immediately received his sight and followed Jesus, praising God. When all the people *saw* it, they also praised God (Luke 18:38-43).

Zacchaeus climbed a tree, for he wanted to *see* who Jesus was (Luke 19:2).

The angels invited the women at the tomb to "Come and *see* the place where He lay... then go quickly and tell... there you will *see* Him" (Matt. 28:5-10).

Mary Magdalene later proclaimed to the incredulous disciples, "I have *seen* the Lord!" (John 20:18).

Prayer:
Father, as an eyewitness of Your majesty, might I, with all urgency, invite others to "Come and *see*."

Psalm 67: The Face of Christ

Focus Verse:	New Testament Verse:
May God be gracious to us and bless us and make his face shine upon us, that your ways may be known on earth, (1, 2a)	For God, who said, "Let light shine out of darkness," made his light shine in our hearts to give us the light of the knowledge of the glory of God in the face of Christ.
	2 Corinthians 4:6

The psalmist, in this beautiful song of blessing, expresses his longing for the light of God's gracious presence to penetrate the darkness of our confused lives in order that:
- ❖ Your ways may be known on Earth, Your salvation among *all* nations
- ❖ That *all* the peoples praise You
- ❖ That the nations of the earth will be guided by the Lord and *all* the ends of the earth will fear You.

Imagine generation after generation of people longingly singing these words accompanied by the beautiful music of stringed instruments. Generation after generation learning anew that it is only a life lived in accordance with His perfect purpose and plan and in dependence upon His perfect provision that leads to joy. For it is God alone who is able to rule men in such a way as to result in gladness, joy, justice, and blessings for *all* peoples of *all* nations.

Prayer:
O Lord, haste the day when faith will be sight... We repeat this prayer again in our generation, for the times are dark and troubled. We desperately need the light of

Your presence. Thank You for sending Jesus to give us the light of the knowledge of Your glory.

Psalm 68: Shining Gold

Focus Verse:	New Testament Verse:
Praise be to the LORD, to God our Savior, who daily bears our burdens. (19)	For you were once darkness, but now you are light in the Lord. Live as children of light (for the fruit of the light consists in all goodness, righteousness and truth)
	Ephesians 5:8, 9

He daily bears the burdens of:
- ❖ The embattled
- ❖ The righteous navigating through a wicked world and a labyrinth of evil
- ❖ The orphaned
- ❖ The widowed
- ❖ The lonely
- ❖ The prisoner
- ❖ The weary
- ❖ The poor

Even while you sleep among the campfires the wings of my dove are sheathed with silver, its feathers with shining gold (v. 13).
For the Lord's "procession has come into view" (v. 24).

Can I, even in the midst of dark valleys, deep confusion, troubling times, battles of the soul, yet experience Your shining presence, may I look up and glimpse, even if fleetingly, Your procession coming into view? I know the answer to that is "yes," for I have experienced this gilding of silver and gold, this glimpse of Your procession coming into view in some of the darkest and most desperate days. These verses are among the gems in my treasure house of precious promises from Your Word. For You daily perfectly provide as we pray, "Give us this day our daily bread."

How lovely, that later in the day on the church bulletin cover, this verse appeared, so fitting, to this Psalm:

"Arise, shine; For thy light is come. And the glory of the Lord is risen upon Thee" (Isa. 60:1).

Prayer:

Thank You, Father. So today, I extend this prayer to troubled believers the world over that they be given a glimpse of Your procession coming into view... that their darkest moments may gleam with the brightest light. That they might see truly that He that is with me is more than those that are with them.

_____
_____
_____
_____
_____
_____
_____
_____

Psalm 69: Deep Waters

Focus Verse:	New Testament Verse:
I am worn out calling for help; my throat is parched. My eyes fail, looking for my God. (3)	In the same way, the Spirit helps us in our weakness. We do not know what we ought to pray for, but the Spirit himself intercedes for us with groans that words cannot express. Romans 8:26

How deep the pain and incapacitating the fear of this suffering servant of the Most High, as he flounders in miry depths where there is no foothold and deep waters and floods are engulfing him.

How far away, how unreachable God can seem in these times of profound suffering. Yet the psalmist steadfastly seeks His sure salvation, His great love, His drawing near to rescue. This is the soul clinging, and though he cannot feel it, as we learned in Psalm 63, the very clinging is only possible as the right hand of his God upholds him.

The beautiful, tender words of our God, expressing His great love and provision for us, spoken through His faithful prophet Isaiah, are so fitting here:

> *Fear not, for I have redeemed you; I have summoned you by name; you are mine. When you pass through the waters, I will be with you; and when you pass through the rivers, they will not sweep over you. When you walk through the fire, you will not be burned; the flames will not set you ablaze. For I am the Lord, your God, the Holy One of Israel, your Savior.* (Isa. 43:1-3)

How we must pray for and encourage our suffering fellow believers who are now floundering in these deep waters. Sometimes when words escape us, the words of our Lord's Prayer fit best.

Prayer:
"Our Father, who art in heaven…"
And as we pray, the precious Holy Spirit comes alongside, interceding on our behalf with groans that words cannot express.

Psalm 70: Just in Time

Focus Verse:	New Testament Verse:
Yet I am poor and needy; come quickly to me, O God. You are my help and my deliverer; O LORD, do not delay. (5)	And he who searches our hearts knows the mind of the Spirit, because the Spirit intercedes for the saints in accordance with God's will. Romans 8:27

The psalmist, David, again in grave danger at the hands of vindictive enemies seeking to kill him, cries out urgently to his God:

- ❖ Hasten
- ❖ Come quickly
- ❖ Do not delay

Father, I pray this prayer of desperation for my fellow believers in my life and around the globe who are:

- ❖ Embattled
- ❖ Imprisoned
- ❖ Persecuted
- ❖ Fleeing
- ❖ Gravely ill
- ❖ Depressed

For this prayer of David, though imperfectly expressed (for You are ever near, always on time, and never delayed), so echoes the heart cries of the human sojourner in our sinful world. And our loving Father, full of grace and truth, translates our troubled pleas into the perfect petition that our own words could not express. For He who searches our hearts knows the mind of the Spirit (Rom. 8:26-27).

Prayer:

Father, thank You that You take even our flawed prayers and turn them into the perfect petition, for You know our hearts just as You knew Your servant David's heart. Father, help us to faithfully bear one another's burdens so that when they are too close to the situation, too desperate to even pray, that others intercede on their behalf, and our troubled prayers, perfectly translated, reach the very throne of grace, ever sufficient to meet us in our time of need.

Psalm 71: Our Legacy

Focus Verse:	New Testament Verse:
Since my youth, O God, you have taught me, and to this day I declare your marvelous deeds. (17)	But as for you, continue in what you have learned and have become convinced of, because you know those from whom you learned it, and how from infancy you have known the holy Scriptures, which are able to make you wise for salvation through faith in Christ Jesus. 2 Timothy 3:14,15

How full of rich treasures is this Psalm written by a psalmist who is reflecting on a lifetime of marvelous teaching. The psalmist looks ahead to more years of being taught, until, even when old and gray, he might yet declare God's power and might to the next generation and to all who are yet to come. What a vision.

Father, I too have sat at Your footstool, learning of You since a young child. I have myself taught children, written cards, kept prayer and devotional journals, sharing and declaring Your marvelous deeds. You have walked with me, and I have sought to keep step with You through all the seasons of my life so far as You have taught me, through Your precious Holy Spirit, precept upon precept, line upon line, these treasured teachings. Lately I have been thinking more and more about how important it is to pass these treasured teachings on to the next generation. In this Psalm, the faithful sojourner seems to be presently walking through a dark valley, yet steadfastly believes his God will *"restore my life again; from the depths of the earth*

You will bring me up and will increase my honor and comfort me once again" (vv. 20-21).

Though we know not its measure (v. 15), for we now see through a glass darkly, may we faithfully tell of Your righteousness and salvation and declare Your power and Your might to the next generation.

Prayer:
The next generation needs to hear not just Your Word, but the experiences of those who have found Your Word to be ever faithful and true. Equip me for the task.

Psalm 72: Intercession for Faulty Leaders

Focus Verse:	New Testament Verse:
May people ever pray for him and bless him all day long. (15b)	I urge, then, first of all, that requests, prayers, intercession and thanksgiving be made for everyone- for kings and all those in authority, that we may live peaceful and quiet lives in all godliness and holiness. 1 Timothy 2:1, 2

This Psalm is a prayer by David for his son Solomon as Solomon becomes king.

Until the future reign of Christ, no matter who is king, president, emperor, dictator, or prime minister, the earth will experience:

- ❖ Injustice
- ❖ Affliction
- ❖ Neediness
- ❖ Oppression
- ❖ Violence

For it is God and God alone who does marvelous deeds. The whole earth *will be* filled with His glory. Until that day of the true theocracy, how important that we faithfully pray for, uphold, and support our leaders as David did here for his son.

In his letter to his young protégé, Timothy, the apostle Paul urged him to pray, intercede, and give thanks for all people, including kings and all those in authority, that we may live peaceful and quiet lives in all godliness and holiness (1 Tim. 2;1-2). It is important to realize the leader of the vast Roman Empire at the time that Paul's letter was dispatched was none other than the wicked emperor Nero, who viciously persecuted Christians in the most horrific ways, including Paul, who was soon martyred. Nevertheless, Paul urged prayer for *all* in authority, and that included Nero.

Preacher Charles Spurgeon is quoted as saying, "prayer is the slender nerve that moves the omnipotent muscle of God" (Spurgeon, 1971). God has in the past and will yet use those whom He chooses to accomplish His perfect plan, as He did the wicked Pharaoh in the time of the exodus. *For Scripture says to Pharaoh: "I raised you up for this very purpose, that I might display my power in you and that my name might be proclaimed in all the earth"* (Rom. 9:17).

Prayer:
O Father, would You endow our leaders, as imperfect as they may be, with your justice and your righteousness. May they lead and speak with righteousness, defend the afflicted, save the needy, and crush the oppressor. Remind us to faithfully lift them up in prayer and bless them, day in and day out. Thy kingdom come, Thy will be done on Earth (even now) as it is in heaven.

This last Psalm of Book II concludes the prayers of David, son of Jesse (v. 20).

Psalm 73: Changing Viewpoints

Focus Verse:	New Testament Verse:
When I tried to understand all this, it was oppressive to me till I entered the sanctuary of God; then I understood their final destiny. (16, 17)	And this is the testimony: God has given us eternal life, and this life is in his Son. He who has the Son has life; he who does not have the Son of God does not have life. 1 John 5:11, 12

The psalmist Asaph begins this third collection of Psalms, the Levitical section, protesting the apparent prosperity, ease, freedom from burden and struggle, pride, arrogance, callous threats, evil conceits, scoffing, and flouting in the face of God of the wicked. The more Asaph thought about it, as for others, the more oppressive it became to him:

Until
I entered the sanctuary of God
Then I understood.

What happened?

Asaph's view changed. His perspective shifted from a localized, limited, here-and-now view of his chaotic world to the view from God's sanctuary, allowing him to see through the temporal to the eternal. With God is life and light and love; without is death, darkness, and hate. "For he who has the Son has life, and he who does not have the Son (no matter what else he may appear to have from an earthly, materialistic perspective) does not have life." Asaph could see what slippery ground the arrogant tread upon. How suddenly will they be destroyed, completely swept away by terrors (vv. 18-19).

Prayer:
Father, strengthen the eyes of my heart that I may see rightly and understand as did Asaph, eventually. Yet I am always with You; You hold me by my right hand. You guide me with Your counsel, and afterward You will take me into glory. Whom have I in heaven but You? And Earth has nothing I desire besides You. My flesh and my heart may fail, but God is the strength of my heart and my portion forever (23-26).

Psalm 74: More Than Conquerors

Focus Verse:	New Testament Verse:
But You, O God, are my king from of old; you bring salvation upon the earth. (12)	No, in all these things we are more than conquerors through him who loved us.
	Romans 8:37

In spite of apparent:
- ❖ Rejection
- ❖ Ruin
- ❖ Destruction
- ❖ Defilement
- ❖ The absence of any miraculous signs
- ❖ Abandonment by the prophets
- ❖ Mockery by enemies
- ❖ Revilement of God's name by foes
- ❖ The holding back of God's hand

But (12)

Yet

Nevertheless

Regardless

You, O God, are my King from of old; You bring salvation upon the earth.

The eyes of faith look through the physically visible dire circumstances and see He who is with us is greater than those who are with them.

For no:
- ❖ Trouble
- ❖ Hardship
- ❖ Persecution
- ❖ Famine

- ❖ Nakedness
- ❖ Danger
- ❖ Sword
- ❖ Death
- ❖ Life
- ❖ Angels
- ❖ Demons
- ❖ The present
- ❖ The future
- ❖ Any powers
- ❖ Height
- ❖ Depth
- ❖ Anything

Will be able to separate us from the love of God that is in Christ Jesus (Rom. 8:38-39).

Thus we pray victoriously with Asaph:

Prayer:
"But you O God, are my King from of old; you bring salvation upon the earth."

Psalm 75: A Solid Foundation

Focus Verse:	New Testament Verse:
You say, "I choose the appointed time; it is I who judge uprightly. (2)	Nevertheless, God's solid foundation stands firm, sealed with this inscription: "The Lord knows those who are his," and "Everyone who confesses the name of the Lord must turn away from wickedness." 2 Timothy 2:19

Thus, we, His people, give thanks, for:
- ❖ His Name is near
- ❖ His timing is perfect
- ❖ His judgment upright.

Even when our physical Earth and all who are in it are quaking, we can have steadfast faith in the faithful one who yet holds its pillars firm (v. 3).

How desperately our confused world needs such a sure foundation. Paul, in his letter to the young Timothy as he began his ministry, shares a word of encouragement with him that yet is true for troubled believers today. In spite of rapidly spreading false teaching, "Nevertheless, God's solid foundation stands firm, sealed with this inscription, 'The Lord knows who are His'" (2 Tim. 2:19).

How solid a foundation is Your Word for our troubled times. In spite of ever-spreading deluded thinking, intolerance for the truth, ridicule of the righteous, and spreading persecution, Your powerful Word yet stands firm.

Prayer:
Father, thank You that You know who belongs to You. You know. You equip us to turn away from the rampant wickedness that surrounds us.

Psalm 76: Splendid Light

Focus Verse:	New Testament Verse:
You are resplendent with light; more majestic than mountains rich with game. (4)	The true light that gives light to every man was coming into the world. John 1:9

In the midst of:
- ❖ Flashing arrows, shields and swords, the weapons of war
- ❖ Valiant men and warriors
- ❖ Horses and chariots

You alone are to be feared.

No one, not even the most valiant warrior, can stand before Your anger, for even the land feared and was quiet.

Your light overcomes.

Your judgment silences.

Your rebuke stills.

Holy, holy, holy. The whole earth is filled with Your glory. As sung in the wonderful hymn, *"Tis only the splendor of light hideth Thee"* (Immortal, Invisible, God Only Wise, Walter Chalmers Smith).

The true light that gives light to every man was coming into the world (John 1:9).

Prayer:

Father, thank You for bringing Your light into the world that we might see. For You have made Your light shine in our hearts to give us the light of the knowledge of the glory of God in the face of Christ.

Psalm 77: A Path Through the Sea

Focus Verse:	New Testament Verse:
Then I thought, "To this I will appeal: the years of the right hand of the Most High," (10)	Not only so, but we also rejoice in our sufferings, because we know that suffering produces perseverance, perseverance, character; and character, hope. And hope does not disappoint us, because God has poured out his love into our hearts by the Holy Spirit, who he has given us. Romans 5:3, 4, 5…

On nights of distress when the soul refuses to be comforted and is too troubled to pray or to even speak, when one begins to wonder if the unfailing love has vanished forever, or if His promises have run out and He has forgotten to be merciful…

Then I thought...

It is then that it occurred to the fainting psalmist what must be done:

I will appeal to the years of the right hand of the Most High.

What a beautiful declaration, so full of hope, faith, and love. The troubled psalmist begins to recount *to God*, to his great and holy God, His ways, His miracles, His mighty deeds; as if to remind God and to hold God to His ways. But in this recounting, the psalmist's spirit is revived and his faith strengthened. It dawns on him in a flash of insight and he declares incredulously: *Your path led through the sea, your way through the mighty waters, though your footprints were not seen* (v. 19).

Sometimes, in fact, God leads us not around the trouble, but instead, straight through the trouble on a most unlikely path (as He did the Israelites through the Red Sea). Most of those times His footprints will not be seen until the eyes of faith begin to focus later, often much later.

Prayer:
Father, may I keep in lockstep with You even through the most troubled path when Your footprints are not seen. May I, like the psalmist, revive my flagging faith by recalling **to You** (thus to me) the years of the right hand of the Most High.

Psalm 78: Pass It On

Focus Verse:	New Testament Verse:
We will not hide them from their children; we will tell the next generation the praiseworthy deeds of the LORD, his power, and the wonders he has done. (4)	Then little children were brought to Jesus for him to place his hands on them and pray for them. But the disciples rebuked those who brought them. Jesus said, "Let the little children come to me, and do not hinder them, for the kingdom of heaven belongs to such as these."
	Matthew 19:13, 14

How important is our spiritual heritage, following His command that we teach our children, so the next generation would know them, even the children yet to be born, who in turn will tell their children so that they should set their hope in God and not forget the works of God, but keep His commandments (v. 6).

Our next generation includes nearly thirty nieces, nephews, spouses, and children. Though we are apart most of the year, show me how I can continually share with them not just Your commands, but the way You have been faithfully teaching me over the years, to recount to them Your praiseworthy deeds, the way I have seen You work in my own life and in the life of my fellow sojourners, to share books and stories with them recounting experiences of great Christians, giants of faith, who have persevered in spite of relentless trials.

The same for the church children I have taught in the past, who are all grown up now with their own children. Father, help us all to be faithful to the recounting. Especially in this time when truth has been so trampled upon and distorted. Help us to hold the bright light of Your Word, Your praiseworthy deeds, Your power, and Your wonders high, so that in the years to come Your truth will yet shine brightly for those not yet born.

Prayer:

Father, I pray for the Stauffer generations. For Aleah, Alex, Amanda, Amber, Anita, Annie, Austin, Ben, Brenda, Bob, Dan H., Dan M., Danae, Dave, Dawn, Dora, Drew, Emily, Emma, Jack, Janice, Jay, Josiah, Julie, Kate Emmaline, Katy, Kyle, Larissa, Luke, Malarie, Mark, Melody, Micah, Nick, Owen, Pete, Phillip, Shannon, Steve, Sylvia, Tim, and Wes. May I never hinder, but instead bring all the little ones (and the grown up ones too) to Jesus.

Psalm 79: A Desperate Prayer

Focus Verse:	New Testament Verse:
May Your mercy come quickly to meet us, for we are in desperate need (8b)	Therefore we do not lose heart. Though outwardly we are wasting away, yet inwardly we are being renewed day by day. For our light and momentary troubles are receiving for us an eternal glory that far outweighs them all. 2 Corinthians 4:16, 17

A desperate prayer then, a desperate prayer now for our troubled, angry, and confused country. I read this Psalm as it happens, on Christmas Eve, as we celebrate the birth of the ultimate gift of mercy that came in the form of a baby, born to die to save us from our sins. How critical that in the midst of our celebrations, we pray for cold hearts to be softened, stubborn minds opened, deaf ears tuned to hear to receive this child king to be their Savior. It was Christmas during the Civil War when Henry Wadsworth Longfellow, in distress over the struggles of the war, sitting at the bedside of his own gravely injured son, penned the words of "I heard the bells on Christmas Day," including these verses:

I heard the bells on Christmas Day
Their old, familiar carols play,
and wild and sweet
The words repeat
Of peace on earth, good-will to men!

And thought how, as the day had come,

The belfries of all Christendom
Had rolled along
The unbroken song
Of peace on earth, good-will to men!

Till ringing, singing on its way,
The world revolved from night to day,
A voice, a chime,
A chant sublime
Of peace on earth, good-will to men!

Then from each black, accursed mouth
The cannon thundered in the South,
And with the sound
The carols drowned
Of peace on earth, good-will to men!

It was as if an earthquake rent
The hearth-stones of a continent,
And made forlorn
The households born
Of peace on earth, good-will to men!

And in despair I bowed my head;
"There is no peace on earth," I said;
"For hate is strong,
And mocks the song
Of peace on earth, good-will to men!"

Then pealed the bells more loud and deep:
"God is not dead, nor doth He sleep;
The Wrong shall fail,

The Right prevail,
With peace on earth, good-will to men." (Longfellow, 1865)

Prayer:
Thank You, Heavenly Father, for Jesus.

_____
_____
_____
_____
_____
_____
_____
_____

Psalm 80: Seeing God

Focus Verse:	New Testament Verse:
Restore us, O God; make Your face shine upon us, that we may be saved. (3, 7, 19)	For our God who said, "Let light shine out of darkness," made his light shine in our hearts to give us the light of the knowledge of the glory of God in the face of Christ.
	2 Corinthians 4:6

What a heartfelt prayer then for the wayward people of Israel, God's chosen ones who so badly needed His restoration and grace. How fitting yet it is as a prayer for our nation today and for the church across the globe. For we, who are of the flock of the Shepherd of Israel, are in need of a Savior, "the Man at your right hand" to awake us to return to You that we may be restored to You. It is through Jesus Christ, the light that shines out of darkness, that God shines in our heart to give us the light of the glory of God that we may be saved (2 Cor. 4:6).

How beautifully this Psalm illustrates the intertwining of the Old and the New. How amazing the God-given vision of this psalmist from years back, looking forward to the cross.

Prayer:
Restore us, oh God; make Your face shine upon us that we may be saved.

Psalm 81: He Gave Them Over

Focus Verse:	New Testament Verse:
So I gave them over to their stubborn hearts to follow their own devices. (12)	Therefore God gave them over in the sinful desires of their hearts... Romans 1:24

Asaph begins this Psalm with songs of joy, shouts of praise, and melodious music. As Asaph recounts Israel's history, he progresses to the warning in the verse selected. Their Lord had:

- ❖ Removed the burden of slavery in Egypt (bondage to sin)
- ❖ Rescued them when they called out in distress, answering them out of thick thunderclouds shrouding Mt. Sinai in the desert of Sin (Exod. 19:16-19).
- ❖ Tested them at the waters of Meribah (which means quarreling); this spot was also called Massah, which means testing (Exod. 17:7).

The Psalm continues, with God speaking, "But My people would not listen to Me, would not submit to Me, and would not follow My way." So God gave them over to their own devices, just like Paul describes years later in his letter to the Roman believers (Rom. 1).

God gave them over in:
- ❖ The sinful desires of their hearts
- ❖ Their shameful lusts
- ❖ Their depraved minds (Rom. 1:24).

What a warning for us as a nation today, as the church throughout the world, and for each of us as individual believers. In previous Psalms we have had an opportunity to repeatedly and in detail remember and recount the ways of God, His miracles, and His mighty deeds.

Prayer:
Oh Father, break through our stony, stubborn hearts, replace them with hearts of flesh; fill them with Your precious Holy Spirit that we might sing songs of joy, shout your praises, and play melodious music as we worship You in spirit and in truth. Move us to follow Your decrees. Save us from our uncleanness. Resettle our towns, rebuild our homes, replant what was desolate (Ezek. 36:26-38).
This new year, oh Father, have Your way in every heart as we daily work in cooperation with You that Your kingdom may come, Your will may be done (*even today*) on Earth as it is in heaven.

Psalm 82: Working for Justice

Focus Verse:	New Testament Verse:
Rise up, O God, judge the earth, for all the nations are your inheritance. (8)	For he has set a day when he will judge the world with justice by the man he has appointed. He has given proof of this to all men by raising him from the dead.
	Acts 17:31

It is God, and God alone, who judges, and will ultimately judge all with perfect justice. Meanwhile, human judges are appointed to execute justice in keeping with godly principles. In this Psalm, these imperfect, fallible judges are urged to cease defending the unjust and showing partiality to the wicked. They are encouraged instead to defend the cause of the weak, the fatherless, the poor, the oppressed and those with limited understanding. Over and over again in scripture, we read of God's concern for the disadvantaged.

The day will come when our perfect God will rise up and judge all in perfect justice, from the lowest to the highest, including those who from their earthly positions judged the weakest. "For He has set a day when He will judge the world with justice by the Man He has appointed. He has given proof of this to all men by raising Him from the dead" (Acts 17:31). May that day come swiftly, oh God.

Prayer:
Father, today we see rampant injustice. I pray for our leaders, our judges, that Thy kingdom come, Thy will be done on earth (*even today*) as it is in heaven. Give our judges wisdom. May we do our part to work to defend

the disadvantaged, the weak, and the needy. Open our eyes to the opportunities.

___
___
___
___
___
___
___
___

Psalm 83: Praying for Our Persecutors

Focus Verse:	New Testament Verse:
O God, do not keep silent; be not quiet, O God, be not still. (1)	bless those who curse you, pray for those who mistreat you. Luke 6:28

God's enemies are astir with reared heads, forming alliances and plotting cunning conspiracies to destroy God's people and blot out their memory.

The psalmist, Asaph, pleads with God to break His silence, His quietness, and His stillness to act in such a clear and dramatic way through fire, tempest, and storm, so that His own people will be preserved and their enemies, their faces covered with shame, will realize the Lord alone is the Most High over all the earth and thus will seek God's name.

The psalmist here recognizes:
- ❖ Through God and God alone Asaph (the pray-er) and his people will be preserved
- ❖ God will act to execute His perfect will at just the right time
- ❖ God will act in such a way as to not only preserve and protect His own, but to also turn their enemies to Him.

Prayer:
Father, teach us to pray in such a way for those who despitefully use us, for the growing number of persecutors and persecuted across our globe. Help us to trust You to always work on our behalf according to the best timetable, to achieve Your perfect plan. "Forgive us our

debts, as we also have forgiven our debtors. And lead us not into temptation, but deliver us from the evil one" (Matt. 6:12-13).

Psalm 84: Hearts Set on Pilgrimage

Focus Verse:	New Testament Verse:
Blessed are those whose strength is in you, who have set their hearts on pilgrimage. (5)	Therefore, since we are surrounded by such a great cloud of witnesses, let us throw off everything that hinders and the sin that so easily entangles, and let us run with perseverance the race marked out for us. Hebrews 12:1

Even as these pilgrims pass through even the Valley of Baca (the Valley of Weeping), they make it a place of springs. These pilgrims move from strength to strength until each appears before God in Zion (vv. 6-7).

This beautiful Psalm brings to mind the classic, *Pilgrim's Progress,* and the experiences of Christian as he journeys to the Celestial City (Bunyan, 1678). In spite of setbacks, failures, and disappointments, Christian travels until at last, he appears before God in Zion. Though at times traversing through the Valley of the Shadow of Death, the sojourner does give way to fear, but yet knows the Good Shepherd is with him, His rod and staff comforting him. As I meditate on the words of this Psalm, I picture the great temple where the Levite psalmist would have served as doorkeeper. This poet minister saw such profound beauty and tenderness in the simplicity of the sparrow and the swallow nesting near the altar with their young that he recorded it here (v. 3). His position as doorkeeper gave him the opportunity to witness close up the beautiful faithfulness of his fellow sojourners coming to the temple year after year, their hearts set on pilgrimage, offering their sacrifices and their gifts of praise, ever looking forward to the promised Messiah. He was profoundly moved by what he saw and thus records it, probably unaware that the words would serve as an encouragement for future believers centuries later.

I consider my own fellow sojourners of today who themselves, in spite of setbacks, failures, and disappointments, yet faithfully, with praise on their lips and their hearts set on pilgrimage, move onward steadily from strength to strength, knowing with certainty that the daily bread will always be provided. In their steadfast faithfulness, I myself have witnessed how these beautiful believers truly transform the Valleys of Baca into places of springs. It is not that they do not weep but that they do not weep as one who has no hope. And they do not weep alone.

Prayer:
Oh Lord Almighty, blessed is the man who trusts in You (v. 12).

Psalm 85: Prepare the Way for His Steps

Focus Verse:	New Testament Verse:
Righteousness goes before him and prepares the way for his steps. (13)	For the eyes of the Lord are on the righteous and his ears are attentive to their prayer,
	1 Peter 3:12a

The psalmist, a Levite, begins his prayer for his people with praise, recounting what God has done on their behalf (and so should we as pray for our own people, our nation today).

Praise:
- ❖ You showed favor to Your land
- ❖ You restored the fortunes of Jacob
- ❖ You forgave the iniquity of Your people and covered all their sins
- ❖ You set aside all Your wrath and turned away from Your fierce anger.

The psalmist next transitions to heartfelt petitions flowing out of his worship, his now clarified view of his God.

Petition:
- ❖ Restore us again
- ❖ Revive us again
- ❖ Show us Your unfailing love
- ❖ Grant us Your salvation.

The psalmist then listens to what God has to say.

Prophecy:
- ❖ There is a promise of peace, but the people must not return to their folly.

- ❖ Salvation is near *those who fear Him* and will lead to the Lord's glory dwelling in the land.
- ❖ The Lord will indeed give what is good; as faithfulness springs up from the earth and righteousness looks down from heaven, there will be a harvest of love and peace.
- ❖ *Righteousness will prepare the way for His steps.*

What if we as a nation corporately, and each of us individually, prayed progressively from praise to petition, then stopped and listened to what God has to say? We can trust that God has in store His perfect provision and plan for our nation, for the church at large, and for our individual lives. Righteousness will prepare the way for His steps.

Prayer:
Father, prepare me to prepare the way for You to move in our midst.

_____
_____
_____
_____
_____
_____
_____

Psalm 86: An Undivided Heart

Focus Verse:	New Testament Verse:
Teach me your way, O LORD, and I will walk in your truth; give me an undivided heart that I may fear Your name. (11)	For to me, to live is Christ and to die is gain. Philippians 1:21
	For you died, and your life is now hidden with Christ in God. Colossians 3:3
	And he died for all, that those who live should no longer live for themselves, but for him who died for them and was raised again. 2 Corinthians 5:15

Again in this Psalm we see the beautiful intertwining of pleading and praising so typical of David. Thus the selected verse is all the more poignant. For this is a pray-er who deeply desires to make God's promises the foundation of his life, the principles by which his life is governed in every aspect. In other words, David is no longer willing to live a segmented life. Instead, he desires for God to be first in his life, in the center, on the throne, ever-present, always in the lead, and guiding every decision. David is figuring out that until he has an undivided heart, it is not possible to truly fear God. Until then, it is all pretend.

David is weary of duplicity, hypocrisy, and half-heartedness. For him, it is all or nothing. It is now or never. And in this psalm, you sense David is all in. Sold out. Hand to the plow. Never looking back.

Father, this touches me. It hits a tender spot. I plead as I often have, Father, do whatever it takes in my life. You can give me a soft heart, a united heart, a whole heart, even a broken heart, but Father, please, at any cost, do not let me have a divided heart. I can no longer live that way. I am tired of holding out, sick of halfway, weary of having a form of godliness but denying its power. I am either in or I am out.

Prayer:
God, I'm through with me. I am ready for You and You alone. It is now or never.

Psalm 87: A Song of Triumph

Focus Verse:	New Testament Verse:
Indeed, of Zion it will be said, "This one and that one were born in her, and the Most High himself will establish her." (5)	Now we see but a poor reflection as in a mirror; then we shall see face to face. Now I know in part; then I shall know fully even as I am fully known.
	1 Corinthians 13:12

What a wondrous time this will be! The future reign of Jesus Christ, the kingdom of God on Earth on the Holy Mountain, Jerusalem. It is incredible to read the registry of the peoples recorded in this Psalm. *I will record Rahab and Babylon among those who acknowledge me–Philistia too and Tyre, along with Cush–and will say, "This one was born in Zion"* (v. 4).

Only the Most High could establish such a city, the City of God, where even former enemies acknowledge Him. "This one was born in Zion."

The Psalm concludes:

As they make music they will sing, "All my fountains are in you" (v. 7).

Prayer:
Father, how eagerly we wait for the day when our faith will be sight when Your Kingdom is established on Earth. What a beautiful song of celebration and triumph. How we hope in You.

Psalm 88: Persistent Prayer

Focus Verse:	New Testament Verse:
O LORD, the God who saves me, day and night I cry out before you. (1)	Then Jesus told his disciples a parable to show them that they should always pray and not give up. Luke 18:1

This Psalm, this prayer of a deeply suffering soul, yet calling out to his God, speaks of a tenacious spirit, of one who, even while his soul is full of trouble, and by his description he is:

- ❖ Drawing near the grave
- ❖ Counted among those who go down to the pit
- ❖ Devoid of strength
- ❖ Set aside with the dead to be remembered no more in the darkest depths, confined and unable to escape
- ❖ Repulsive to his closest friends; in fact, darkness has become his closest friend…

Yet calls to the Lord every day and all through the night, spreading out his hands to God.

A parable Jesus told comes to mind, recorded in Luke 18. Jesus told His disciples the purpose of the parable was to illustrate they should always pray and never give up. The widow in the story returned time and time again to the unjust judge, persistently pleading that he grant her justice against her adversary. Eventually her request was granted, not because the uncaring judge wished to render justice, but because he wanted peace and quiet. Jesus reasoned that since this self-centered judge eventually granted the widow her request so she would quit bothering him, how much more will God bring about justice, and quickly, for *His chosen ones,* who cry out to Him day and night?

Jesus ends His parable with a thought-provoking question, "However, when the Son of Man comes, will He find faith on the earth?"

We should ask ourselves, "How persistent are we willing to be in prayer?" Are we willing to ask and keep asking, to knock and keep knocking, to seek and keep seeking, even when there is no response, no doors opening, no finding; even when, especially when the situation is dark and desperate? If ever there was a time when we needed to be persistent in prayer, it is now, for ourselves, for our churches, for our communities, for our country, and for our world. When Jesus returns, will any of us be on our knees, persistently pleading

Prayer:
Father, I know prayer changes things. Help me to pray and never give up. Ever.

Psalm 89: Ceaseless Praise

Focus Verse:	New Testament Verse:
Praise be to the LORD forever! Amen and Amen. (52)	Through Jesus, therefore, let us continually offer to God a sacrifice of praise–the fruit of lips that confess his name.
	Hebrews 13:15

With this expression of praise, the psalmist concludes this Psalm, and with this Psalm, Book III of the Psalms concludes. *Praise be to the Lord forever! Blessed (happy) indeed are those who have learned to acclaim you, who walk in the light of your presence, O Lord* (v. 15).

What a beautiful thought this is. We can learn to be praise-ers on even the darkest of dark days, to in fact, on those darkest of days, learn to follow hard after You, to keep in step with You, so that we are, in fact, walking in the light of Your presence. Because regardless of our present and immediate earthly circumstances that can tend to frighten and overwhelm us, we can learn, by training the eyes of our heart, to focus not on what is seen, but unseen.

G. Campbell Morgan shares this comforting illumination of this Psalm:

> Thus the soul who has come to a knowledge of God as the Mighty-Helper will worship Him in a perpetual doxology on the darkest day, remembering His covenant, and being assured that whatever may be the experiences of the moment, in the long issue He will be vindicated. Thus

the men of faith render Him ceaseless worship.
(Morgan, 1994)

Prayer:
Father, I pray I will reach the point where every moment of my life flows in ceaseless praise to You, my God, my Redeemer. Teach me to acclaim You.

Psalm 90: Making Our Days Count

Focus Verse:	New Testament Verse:
LORD, you have been our dwelling place throughout all generations. (1)	See then that you walk circumspectly, not as fools, but as wise, redeeming the time, because the days are evil.
	Ephesians 5:15, 16 (KJV)

Psalm 90 opens Book IV of the Psalms, the Numbers section. The Psalm is labeled as "a prayer of Moses the man of God." This is the prayer of a humble, faithful (though flawed) servant of the Lord, who, in spite of his amazing life story, rightly saw his life and the life of the people he led against the backdrop of eternity. This man of God was the only man known to be buried by God Himself (Deut. 34).

How gleaming bright and beautiful are the sparkling gems in the storehouse of this treasured Psalm:

Lord, You have been our dwelling place throughout all generations (v. 1).

From everlasting to everlasting You are God (v. 2).

You have set our iniquities before You, our secret sins in the light of Your presence (v. 8).

Teach us to number our days aright, that we may gain a heart of wisdom (v. 12).

Satisfy us in the morning with Your unfailing love that we may sing for joy and be glad all our days (v. 14).

May Your deeds be shown to Your servants, Your splendor to their children (v. 16).

May the favor of the Lord our God rest upon us; establish the work of our hands for us–yes, establish the work of our hands (v. 17).

Our Lord:
    Everlasting
        Light
            Love
                Splendor

Prayer:
Father, in recent months, in this nation, we have experienced tragic, evil attacks in large cities and in a small rural church. We hear about the escalating murder rates in our cities, including Baltimore, three miles up the road from where I write. Abortion, euthanasia, political division, hatred, partisanship, racial and ethnic tensions, sexual harassment, rampant pornography, the worsening opioid epidemic, international tensions, persecution of Christians and intolerance for the truth. Father, as we live out the very verses of Romans 1 in these last days, teach us to number our days right, that we may gain a heart of wisdom, walking carefully, making good use of our time, recognizing the days are evil, and the time short.

_____

_____

_____

_____

_____

_____

_____

Psalm 91: The Secret Place

Focus Verse:	New Testament Verse:
He that dwelleth in the secret place of the Most High shall abide under the shadow of the Almighty. (1) (KJV)	My prayer is not that you take them out of the world but that you protect them from the evil one.
	John 17:15

This Psalm of unknown authorship is closely related to Moses' Psalm preceding it. It is speculated that it was written by some later singer as a personal testimony to the truth of the previous song.

This Psalm is personal and singular in contrast to the plural pronouns of Moses' Psalm. Here, in the KJV, the writer speaks of the secret place. It is through Christ and Christ alone that we are worthy at all to ascend to His holy hill, to dwell (abide) in the place of the Most High. To rest (abide) in the shadow of the Almighty, to be covered by His feathers, and find refuge under His wings, leading to perfect peace, security, and freedom from fear. Confident that no spiritual harm or disaster will befall the one hidden in the secret place.

Again as in Psalm 90, Romans 1 comes to mind. We live in a world that God has abandoned to its own sinful desires, that is in an ever-accelerating downward spiral. Nevertheless, the true follower of Christ is yet equipped to live victoriously, to be instrumental in "Thy kingdom come, Thy will be done on earth as it is in heaven." How fitting the John 17 prayer is here as we consider this Psalm's application to our lives today as we live in a Romans 1 world.

Prayer:
Father, lead us not into temptation, but deliver us from evil.

Psalm 92: An Octave of Praise

Focus Verse:	New Testament Verse:
It is good to praise the LORD and make music to Your name, O Most High, (1)	Speak to one another with psalms, hymns, and spiritual songs. Sing and make music in your heart to the Lord, always giving thanks to God the Father for everything, in the name of our Lord Jesus Christ.
	Ephesians 5:19, 20

G. Campbell Morgan suggests this Psalm " and the seven that follow (92-99) "constitute an octave of perfect praise suitable to the Sabbath Day," with the theme that of the Kingship of Jehovah (Morgan, 1994).

In this Psalm, labeled "A psalm. A song. For the Sabbath day. the emphasis here is living lives bookended with praise, making music to His name, the Most High, and proclaiming His love and His faithfulness in the morning and at night. Continually flourishing and growing as only a planting in the house of the Lord can do, so that even as our earthly journey is drawing to its close, "They will stay fresh and green, proclaiming, 'The Lord is upright, He is my Rock, and there is no wickedness in Him'" (vv. 14-15). A couple verses of a favorite hymn comes to mind and are fitting for this Sabbath Psalm:

> *Take my life and let it be*
> *Consecrated Lord, to thee;*
> *Take my moments and my days;*
> *Let them flow in ceaseless praise,*
> *Let them flow in ceaseless praise.*

Take my voice, and let me sing,
Always only, for my King,
Take my lips and let them be
Filled with message from Thee,
Filled with messages from Thee
(Frances Ridley Havergal, 1874)

Prayer:
Father, my prayer is this: that my life will be consecrated to You; my moments and my days flowing in ceaseless praise to You.

Psalm 93: Pavilioned in Splendor

Focus Verse:	New Testament Verse:
The LORD reign, he is robed in majesty; the LORD is robed in majesty and is armed with strength. (1)	We did not follow cleverly invented stories when we told you about the power and coming of our Lord Jesus Christ, but we were eye witnesses of his majesty. 2 Peter 1:16

How wondrous it is as a child of God, and deeply loved by and cared for by Him, to stop, look up, and realize anew that:
The Lord, my Lord is on the throne.
He is robed in majesty and armed with strength.
He reigns.
His throne was established long ago–from all eternity.
His statutes stand firm.
Holiness adorns His house for endless days.
This will never change. It is firmly established. No cataclysmic weather event can ever reach that throne; no pounding waves, no thundering great waters or breakers of the sea will ever wash over it.
Our Lord reigns.
Again, a remembered hymn for this second of the Sabbath Psalms (92-99). Though based on Psalm 104, it is fitting here as well and serves as our prayer, *O Worship the King*.

Prayer:
> *O Worship the King all glorious above*
> *O gratefully sing His power and His love,*

Our Shield and Defender, the Ancient of Days
Pavilioned in splendor, and girded with praise.

O tell of His might, O sing of His grace,
Whose robe is the light, whose canopy space,
His chariots of wrath the deep thunderclouds form,
And dark is His path on the wings of the storm.

Thy bountiful care, what tongue can recite?
It breathes in the air, it shines in the light,
It streams from the hills, it descends to the plain,
And sweetly distills on the dew and the rain.
(Robert H. Grant, 1833)

Psalm 94: Though the Wrong Seem Oft So Strong

Focus Verse:	New Testament Verse:
They say, "The LORD does not see; the God of Jacob pays no heed." (7)	Praise be to the God and Father of our Lord Jesus Christ, the Father of compassion and the God of all comfort, who comforts us in all our troubles, so that we can comfort those in any trouble with the comfort we ourselves have received from God. For just as the sufferings of Christ flow over into our lives, so also through Christ our comfort overflows.
	2 Corinthians 1:3-5
	May the God of hope fill you with all joy and peace as you trust in him, so that you may overflow with hope by the power of the Holy Spirit.
	Romans 15:13

Here in this third Psalm of the octet of Sabbath praise songs (92-99), the psalmist has shifted his perspective from the majestic throne to the wickedness all around him. He has not lost that view of the throne; instead, with that throne in mind, he is thinking now of the foolishness of the wicked as evidenced by their arrogant words, their boasting, their crushing acts of oppression in regards to God's inheritance, the widows, the aliens, and the fatherless.

The wicked claim, "The Lord does not see or pay heed." Our psalmist now considers the perspective of the Lord on the throne toward these wicked, senseless fools:

❖ Does He who implanted the ear not hear?

- ❖ Does He who formed the eye not see?
- ❖ Does He who disciplines nations not punish?
- ❖ Does He who teaches man lack knowledge?
- ❖ The Lord knows the thoughts of man; He knows they are futile.

By contrast, those the Lord disciplines and teaches are blessed as God protects and cares for them-even as the wicked seem to triumph.

I love the triumphant third verse of "This is My Father's World":

> *This is my Father's world, O let me ne'er forget*
> *That though the wrong seem oft so strong,*
> *God is the ruler yet.*
> *This is my Father's world:*
> *The battle is not done,*
> *Jesus, who died shall be satisfied,*
> *And heav'n and earth be one.*
> *Amen.*
> (Malthie D. Babcock, 1901)

Prayer:

Father, I pray for those who are yet trusting You in the darkest of situations: the persecuted of Your inheritance, the disadvantaged (widowed, orphaned, the refugee). Give them help. Support them with Your love even as they are slipping. Console them and give them joy in the midst of their greatest anxiety. Remind them anew that this is Your world. And that though the wrong seems so strong, *you are the ruler yet.*

Psalm 95: Reverence

Focus Verse:	New Testament Verse:
Come, let us bow down in worship, let us kneel before the LORD our maker. (6)	to the only God our Savior be glory, majesty, power and authority, through Jesus Christ our Lord, before all ages, now and forevermore! Amen.
	Jude 25

In this fourth of the octet of Sabbath Psalms (92-99), the theme is the greatness of our Jehovah King, and in this verse, the right response then of the created to their Creator King.

Joy, yes. Even shouts, music, and songs of thanksgiving. But also reverence. Always reverence.

For our God is the Most High (Ps. 92).

He is majestic, armed with strength; He is holy (Ps. 93).

He is a God who hears, sees, disciplines, and teaches (Ps. 94).

Our Lord is the great God, the great King, above all gods (Ps. 95).

He holds the depths of the earth in the palm of one hand, while yet capping the mountain peaks with the other. The seas are His, for He made them and His hands formed the dry land.

He made us and we are His people of His pasture, the flock under His care.

A hymn of remembrance to fit with this Sabbath Psalm is one I can remember my mother singing at times in German. It is our prayer.

Prayer:
Holy God We Praise Thy Name

Holy God we praise Thy Name;
Lord of all, we bow before Thee;
All on earth Thy scepter claim
All in heaven above adore Thee.
Infinite Thy vast domain
Everlasting in Thy reign.
Clarence Augusto Wolworth, 1853 (a German hymn)

_____
_____
_____
_____
_____
_____
_____
_____
_____

Psalm 96: He Comes

Focus Verse:	New Testament Verse:
they will sing before the LORD, for he comes, he comes to judge the earth. (13)	Amen. Come, Lord Jesus. Revelations 22:20b

In this fifth of the octet of Sabbath Psalms (92-99) is a remarkable phrase gleaming with hope: *He comes*.

Our great and glorious God, the creator of the heavens, who reigns in majesty, splendor, strength, and holiness *comes*.

He *comes* to judge the earth.

He will judge the earth in righteousness and the peoples with His truth.

Thus this beautiful song of praise, for... He *comes*.

No wonder then, "the creation waits in eager expectation for the sons of God to be revealed" (Rom. 8:19). We are sons (children) of God because of His great gift of salvation through the blood shed for us by His Son Jesus Christ. Thus, we along with all creation "groan inwardly as we wait eagerly for adoption as sons (children), the redemption of our bodies" (Rom. 8:32).

We eagerly wait for our righteous judge to *come*.

Until that day, we must be urgently proclaiming His salvation; we must be about our Father's business.

My prayer, the hymn, "*Come*, Thou Almighty King":

Prayer:
> *Come, Thou Almighty King.*
> *Help us Thy name to sing,*
> *Help us to praise:*
> *Father, all-glorious,*
> *O'er all victorious,*
> *Come and reign over us,*
> *Ancient of Day.*
> (Anonymous, 1757)

Psalm 97: He is on the Throne

Focus Verse:	New Testament Verse:
Clouds and thick darkness surround him; righteousness and justice are the foundations of his throne. (2)	-God, the blessed, and only Ruler, the King of kings and Lord of lords, who alone is immortal, and who lives in unapproachable light, whom no one has seen or can see. To him be honor and might forever. Amen. 1 Timothy 6:15, 16

This is the sixth of the octet of Sabbath Psalms (92-99).
How wondrous this song is.
How magnificent to remember anew that:
There is a throne in heaven.
There is someone on the throne.
The foundations of the throne are righteousness and justice. So no matter how tumultuous the storm or thick the darkness that momentarily obscures our view of His ways, His purpose, His plan, even His very presence, we know He yet reigns. Whatever His methods, He ever reigns with absolute righteousness; He rules with perfect justice. One day His lightning will light up the world; the earth will tremble; the mountains melt as the heavens proclaim His glory and all the peoples on Earth will see Him as He is.

At that moment, all those who worship at the feet of wealth, power, position, career, creation, and false cults, gods, and idols will suddenly realize with a startling burst of insight that He is the Most High, exalted far above all other gods they have been chasing after.

Also at that moment His light will be shed upon the righteous and joy on the upright in heart.

Prayer:
Father, as I wait for that day, help me to remember on the darkest and stormiest days and nights, 'tis only the splendor of light hideth Thee.

Immortal, Invisible, God

Immortal, invisible, God only wise,
In light inaccessible hid from our eyes
Most blessed, most glorious, the Ancient of Day,
Almighty, victorious, Thy great name we praise.

Unresting, unhasting, and silent as light,
Nor wanting, nor wasting Thou rulest in might;
Thy justice like mountains high soaring above
The clouds which are fountains of goodness and love.

To all, life Thou givest to both great and small;
In all life Thou livest, the true life of all;
We blossom and flourish as leaves on the tree,
And wither and perish, but naught changeth Thee.

Great Father of glory, pure Father of light,
Thine angels adore Thee, all veiling their sight;
All praise we would render; O help us to see
'Tis only the splendor of light hideth Thee.
(Walter Chalmers Smith, 1867)

Psalm 98: The Way Devised

Focus Verse:	New Testament Verse:
Sing to the LORD a new song, for he has done marvelous things; his right hand and his holy arm have worked salvation for him. (1) The LORD has made his salvation known and revealed his righteousness to the nations. (2)	"And he made know to us the mystery of his will according to his good pleasure, which he purposed in Christ to be put into effect when the times will have reached their fulfillment–to bring all things in heaven and on earth together under one head, even Christ. Ephesians 1:9-10

This is the seventh of the octet of Sabbath Psalms (92-99). Indeed, He has done marvelous things. It is the way devised that we may not remain estranged from Him (2 Sam. 14:14).

Our plight as sinners separates us from God as in the mysterious story in 2 Samuel 14 regarding David's banished son, Absalom, "like water spilled out on the ground, which cannot be recovered, so we must die. But God does not take away life; instead, He devises ways so that a banished person may not remain estranged from Him." It was His will that we not remain estranged from Him. It took His plan, His providence, and His power (His right hand and His holy arm) to do what could not be done by human effort, the recovery of "spilled," wasted, sin-ruined lives. Even the way devised would not be enough if He then did not make His salvation known. But He did. He revealed His righteousness to the nations.

> *And He made know to us the mystery of His will–to the praise of His glorious grace according to His good pleasure, which He purposed in Christ to be put into effect when the times will have reached their fulfillment–to bring all things, in heaven and earth under one head, even Christ.* (Ephes. 1:9-10)

Paul describes this way devised, this working of salvation, and the revealing of it in his beautiful letter to the Philippians.

> *Who, being in very nature God, did not consider equality with God something to be used to his own advantage; rather, he made himself nothing by taking the very nature of a servant, being made in human likeness. And being found in appearance as a man, he humbled himself by becoming obedient to death — even death on a cross! Therefore God exalted him to the highest place and gave him the name that is above every name, that at the name of Jesus every knee should bow, in heaven and on earth and under the earth, and every tongue acknowledge that Jesus Christ is Lord, to the glory of God the Father.* (Phil. 2:6-11)

Small wonder then that the entire earth-even the seas, rivers, and mountains-shout for joy, burst into jubilant song, and make music to the Lord.
For He comes.

Prayer (and hymn):
O Come, O Come, Emmanuel.

Psalm 99: At His Footstool

Focus Verse:	New Testament Verse:
Exalt the LORD our God and worship at his footstool; he is holy. (5)	Be imitators of God, therefore, as dearly loved children and live a life of love, just as Christ loved us and gave himself up for us as a fragrant offering and sacrifice to God.
	Ephesians 5:1, 2

This is the final of the suggested octet of Sabbath songs (92-99) praising our Jehovah Lord as the exalted, majestic King reigning on His throne over all the earth. Those who, with stilled hearts and renewed minds are eyewitnesses of His majesty, shake and tremble as they exalt the Lord our God and worship at His footstool. Picture the very Throne Room of the Most High.

He reigns, enthroned between the cherubim (the Holy of Holies).

He, our King, is mighty, loving justice.

He has established equity.

He is holy.

Thus with our eyes focused on the unseen, our minds and affections on things above, with this right view of our God, we exalt Him and worship at His footstool. It is there at the footstool we learn of Him. We find the secret dwelling place of the Most High. We are sheltered under His wings. It is here that we become holy as He is holy, fully protected and cleansed from the corruption of sin.

Near to the Heart of God

There is a place of quiet rest,
Near to the heart of God;
A place where sin cannot molest,
Near to the heart of God.
O Jesus, blest Redeemer,
Sent from the heart of God;
Hold us, who wait before Thee,
Near to the heart of God.
There is a place of comfort sweet,
Near to the heart of God;
A place where we our Savior meet,
Near to the heart of God.
There is a place of full release,
Near to the heart of God;
A place where all is joy and peace,
Near to the heart of God.
(Cleland B. McAfee, 1903)

Prayer:
Father, might I as I learn of You, give my life, as Christ did for me, as a fragrant offering.

Psalm 100: In His Presence

Focus Verse:	New Testament Verse:
Shout for joy to the LORD all the earth. (1)	I have given them the glory that you gave me, that they may be one as we are one. I in them and you in me. May they be brought to complete unity to let the world know that you sent me and have loved them even as you have loved me. Father, I want those you have given me to be with me where I am, and to see my glory, the glory you have given me because you loved me before the creation of the word.
John 17:22-24

Shout for joy to the Lord
Worship with gladness
Come before Him with joyful songs
Know that the Lord is God
It is He who has made us, and we are His
We are His people, the sheep of His pasture
Enter His gates with thanksgiving and His courts with praise
Give thanks to Him and praise His name,
For the Lord is good
His love endures forever;
His faithfulness to all generations.
We begin our *worship* with joy and gladness.
As we *come* before Him, we come to know more deeply who He is and whose we are.
As we *enter* into the Holy of Holies, that secret pace of the Most High, our dwelling place, it is there that we, with unveiled faces, reflect the Lord's glory. It is there that

we are being transformed into His likeness with ever-increasing glory.
It is there and it is then that we *give* thanks and praise His name.

Prayer:
Father, as I daily seek to worship You, to come into Your presence, to know You more deeply as I enter into fellowship with You, giving thanks and praise, may others increasingly see Jesus reflected in me.

_____
_____
_____
_____
_____
_____
_____
_____

Psalm 101: Being Blameless

Focus Verse:	New Testament Verse:
I will walk in my house with blameless heart. I will set before my eyes no vile thing. (2b, 3)	For this very reason, make every effort to add to your faith goodness; and to goodness, knowledge; and to knowledge, self-control; and to self-control, perseverance; and to perseverance, godliness; and to godliness brotherly kindness; and to brotherly kindness, love. 2 Peter 1:5-7

This Psalm of King David is very much the prayer of a ruler and his commitment to ordering both his personal life and that of his administration in harmony with the Most High, King of kings, and Lord of lords. The selected verse emphasizes his decisions regarding his own life and is a good companion to Moses' prayer, "Teach us to order our days aright" (Ps. 90).

It also brings to mind the Old Testament story of Nehemiah and his leadership of the returning exiles in rebuilding the crumbled wall around the destroyed city of Jerusalem. It was a monumental, overwhelming task, fraught with obstacles, challenges, and dangers *until* it was determined that each one would focus on rebuilding their own section of the wall.

What if:

❖ Instead of this endless garment rending about the sorry state of our sinful world today, we each-as David, Moses, and the wall builders did-chose to commit ourselves to a blameless, God-led life, to set before our eyes no vile thing, and to take personal responsibility and accountability to rebuild our own

section of the wall instead of bemoaning the hopeless state of affairs?
- ❖ We, as commanded in 1 Peter 1:15, determined to, with God's grace, be holy as He is holy?
- ❖ We are committed to abstaining from the sinful desires which war against our souls (1 Pet. 2:11)?
- ❖ We made every effort to add to our faith goodness; and to our goodness knowledge; and to knowledge self-control; and to self-control perseverance; and to perseverance godliness; and to godliness brotherly kindness; and to brotherly kindness love (2 Pet. 1:5-7)?

The promise given in this Psalm is this: My eyes will be on the faithful in the land, that they may dwell with Me; he whose walk is blameless, will minister to Me (v. 6).

Prayer:
Father, I want to dwell with You. I want to minister to You. With Your grace, I commit myself as David did to walk before You with a blameless life, no matter the evil circumstances around me.

Psalm 102 (A Penitential Psalm): Begging for Mercy

Focus Verse:	New Testament Verse:
But You remain the same, and your years will never end. The children of your servants will live in your presence; their descendants will be established before you. (27, 28)	But the tax collector stood at a distance. He would not even look up to heaven, but beat his breast and said, 'God, have mercy on me, a sinner.' Luke 18:13

This Psalm is labeled, "A prayer of an afflicted man. When he is faint and pours out his lament before the Lord."

This then is the heartfelt prayer of a soul who recognizes his own role in his ruin, yet humbly cries out to the Lord for help.

This is a man whose strength is broken (v. 23), thus he has come to the end of himself.

It is then, and only then, that many, if not all of us, are ready to lay all on the altar. Like the tax collector in the parable Jesus told, he pleaded for God's mercy while the Pharisee thanked God that he was not like other men, even including, perhaps especially, the tax collector standing nearby.

It is the everlasting changelessness of our God that is our salvation.

- ❖ He yet reigns (v. 12).
- ❖ He yet acts on our behalf, arising to help us (v. 13).
- ❖ He yet shows His compassion at the appointed time (v. 13).
- ❖ He promises to respond to the prayer and plea of the destitute, desperate, and distressed (v. 17).

❖ Our Lord sees, He hears, He acts (vv. 19-20).

Prayer:
You, Lord, remain the same. It is I who strays. I will pray and keep on praying. For as hopeless and desperate as it may seem, You yet see, hear, and act on behalf of the repentant heart. God, have mercy on me, a sinner.

Psalm 103: True Worship

Focus Verse:	New Testament Verse:
Praise the LORD, O my soul; all my inmost being praise his holy name. (1)	Yet a time is coming and has now come when the true worshipers will worship the Father in spirit and truth, for they are the kind of worshipers the Father seeks. God is spirit, and his worshipers must worship in spirit and in truth.
	John 4:23, 24

All my inmost being praises Him as I remember *all* His benefits:
- ❖ He forgives all my sins
- ❖ He heals all my diseases
- ❖ He redeems my life
- ❖ He satisfies my desires
- ❖ He renews my youth
- ❖ He works righteousness and justice for the oppressed
- ❖ He makes known His ways
- ❖ He is compassionate and gracious
- ❖ He is slow to anger
- ❖ He is abounding in love
- ❖ He is merciful
- ❖ He has removed our transgressions away as far as the east is from the west
- ❖ He rules over all.

Fear Him.
Keep His covenant.
Remember to obey His precepts.
It is then, and only then, that my inmost being can truly praise His holy name.

Prayer:
Father, I want to worship You as You desire, in spirit and in truth, in my inmost being. Thank You for making known Your ways to us through Jesus.

Psalm 104: This is My Father's World

Focus Verse:	New Testament Verse:
How many are your works, O LORD! In wisdom you made them all; The earth is full of your creatures. (24)	For by him all things were created: things in heaven and on earth, visible and invisible, whether thrones or powers or rulers or authorities; all things were created by him and for him. He is before all things, and in him all things hold together. Colossians 1:16, 17

What a joyous Psalm this is, overflowing with delight in the marvels of creation. Having just read the Genesis creation account in preparation for a children's Sunday school class, it was a blessing to immediately follow this by reading again these treasured verses, remembering the joy of sharing this Psalm with another class of children many years ago. What fun we had looking for all the different works of creation celebrated in this Psalm. Perhaps this Psalm is best read from the pure, innocent viewpoint of a child.

How wonderful, in the midst of such chaos and confusion, such hatred and ugliness in our world today, to simply sit back and marvel with the psalmist, and with unrestrained joy, praise the Creator and Sustainer of all things. We begin to grasp the Creator's satisfaction in proclaiming each day of creation, that "it was good." The psalmist, in his joyous reveling, calls on his Creator to rejoice in His works (v. 31).

The opening words of the Gospel of John come to mind in all their quivering beauty: *In the beginning was the Word, and the Word was with God, and the Word was God. He was with God at the beginning. Through Him all things were made; without Him, nothing was made that has been made* (John 1:1-3).

As do the words of the apostle Paul in his letter to the Colossians: *For by Him all things were created: things in heaven and on earth, visible and invisible, whether thrones or powers or rulers, or authorities; all things were created for Him and by Him. He is before all things and in Him all things hold together* (Col. 1:16-17).

Prayer:

Father, all I can say is thank you. There is such majesty, such beauty, such power in these verses. I am so glad that I can victoriously proclaim, this is my Father's world.

Psalm 105: Remembering the God Who Remembers

Focus Verse:	New Testament Verse:
Remember the wonders he has done... (5)	It is no trouble for me to write the same things to you again, and it is a safeguard for you.
He remembers his covenant forever, (8)	Philippians 3:1b

How essential to our spiritual well-being and growth that we continually remember the words and ways of the one who remembers.
- ❖ The wonders He has done
- ❖ The miracles He performs
- ❖ The judgments He pronounces

How essential that we look to the Lord and His strength and seek His face always (v. 4).

The psalmist here recounts:
- ❖ The covenant made, sworn to, and confirmed with Abraham, Isaac, and Jacob.
- ❖ The protection and preservation of the Israelites through years of nation wandering, famine, oppression, and ultimately delivery from the land of slavery (Egypt).
- ❖ The perpetual guidance by cloud and fire through the years of wilderness wandering that followed.
- ❖ The daily supplying (the perfect provision).
- ❖ The delivery into the Promised Land.

The purpose:

That they may keep His precepts and observe His laws (v. 45).

Paul wrote to his beloved Philippians, "It is no trouble for me to write the same things to you again, and it is a safeguard for you" (Phil. 3:11).

How I treasure this verse and think of it often in regard to my own need to read God's Word and remember anew His faithfulness. I also think of it in regard to teaching children, relating to fellow believers, and encouraging others.

Prayer:
Father, I need the safeguard of Your life-giving Word, Your rock-solid promises, Your treasured teachings woven into the very fabric of my life that I might always remember and not forget. May I seek Your face always, keeping Your mercy in view.

_____
_____
_____
_____
_____
_____
_____
_____

Psalm 106: Remembering to Remember

Focus Verse:	New Testament Verse:
Who can proclaim the mighty acts of the LORD or fully declare his praise? (2)	Therefore, I urge you, brothers, **in view of God's mercy**, to offer Your bodies as living sacrifices, holy and pleasing to God–this is your spiritual act of worship. Do not conform any longer to the pattern of this world, but be transformed by the renewing of your mind. Then you will be able to test and approve what God's will is–his good, pleasing, and perfect will,
	Romans 12:1, 2

If Psalm 105 is the Psalm of remembering, then Psalm 106 is the Psalm of forgetting. In reading it, we come to understand anew our continual need to be reminded to remember. This is the last Psalm of Book IV, the Numbers section, to be followed by the Deuteronomy section with the theme of remembering.

The answer to the psalmist's question posed in the selected verse is in verse 3: *Blessed are they who maintain justice, who constantly do what is right.*

Then the psalmist recounts in verse after verse the repeated failure of the people, relating their shortcomings to those of their forefathers:

- ❖ They gave no thought to Your miracles (v. 7)
- ❖ They did not remember Your kindness and rebelled (vv. 7-12)
- ❖ Even after a miraculous rescue, they soon forgot what You had done and did not wait for Your counsel (v. 13)
- ❖ They gave into their craving and put You to the test (vv. 14-15)

- ❖ They grew envious of their leaders (vv. 16-18)
- ❖ They exchanged You, their glory, for an image of a bull that eats grass (v. 21)
- ❖ They forgot You, the one who saved them (vv. 21-23)
- ❖ They despised the pleasant land
- ❖ They did not believe the promise
- ❖ They grumbled in their tents
- ❖ They did not obey You
- ❖ They yoked themselves to the Baal of Peor
- ❖ They ate sacrifices offered to lifeless gods (vv. 27-28)
- ❖ They provoked You to anger with their deeds (v. 27)
- ❖ They angered You and rebelled against the Spirit of God
- ❖ They did not destroy completely but mingled with and adopted the customs of the nations, worshiping their idols, even falling into child sacrifice and shedding innocent blood
- ❖ Bent on rebellion, they defiled and prostituted themselves.

The consequences:
- ❖ You gave them what they asked for
- ❖ The earth they were so obsessed with consumed them
- ❖ They wandered in the desert and were ultimately scattered through the lands, living under the rule of their foes
- ❖ They suffered through plagues
- ❖ They were oppressed
- ❖ They wasted away in sin.

The true praise-er is the one who, in the midst of their oppression, coming to their senses, stops to bring God's mercy in view. When giving thought to, in remembering, and in considering their God and all His works on their behalf, they are compelled out of love to a new life of obedience, and thus can truly proclaim the doxology, these closing words of this fourth book of Psalms: *Praise be to the Lord, the God of Israel, from everlasting to everlasting. Let all the people say, "Amen!" Praise the Lord* (v. 48).

How fitting the words of my life verses here, down to the "therefore":

> *Therefore, I urge you, brothers,* in view of God's mercy, *to offer Your bodies as living sacrifices, holy and pleasing to God–this is your spiritual act of worship. Do not conform any longer to the pattern of this world, but be transformed by the renewing of your mind. Then you will be able to test and approve what God's will is–His good, pleasing, and perfect will.* (Rom. 12:1-2)

We must continually keep God's mercy in view.

Prayer:
Remind me, Lord, to remember. Renew my mind. Bring me to my senses.

Psalm 107: He Came

Focus Verse:	New Testament Verse:
Whoever is wise, let him heed these things and consider the great love of the LORD. (43)	The Spirit of the Lord is on me, because he has anointed me to preach good news to the poor. He has sent me to proclaim freedom for the prisoners and recovery of sight for the blind, to release the oppressed, to proclaim the year of the Lord's favor.
	Luke 4:18, 19

With this Psalm, the fifth and final of the Books of Psalms, the Deuteronomy section, opens. The psalmist gives us example after example of the Lord's unfailing love and His wonderful deeds for men for us to consider and give thanks.

Homeless, hungry, thirsty wanderers in a wasteland were delivered and led to a city where they could settle (vv. 4-9).

Therefore God is not ashamed to be called their God, for He has prepared a city for them. (Heb. 11:16)

Prisoners in darkness, deepest gloom, helplessness, subjected to bitter labor for their rebellion against God's Word and despising His counsel, are saved, brought out of the darkness and deepest gloom, unchained, gates broken, and their confining iron bars cut through (vv. 10-16).

He has sent me to proclaim freedom for the prisoners...
- Jesus reading the scroll of the prophet Isaiah in Nazareth (Luke 4:18)

Janice Stauffer MacLeod

The rebels afflicted for iniquities to the point of being unable to eat; they became fools. He sent forth His Word and healed them. He rescued them from the grave (vv. 17-22).

The Word became flesh and made His dwelling among us.
(John 1:14)

When sailors were caught in a raging storm at sea, at their wits' end, reeling and staggering, in response to their cries, He stilled the storm to a whisper and guided them to their desired haven (vv. 23-32).

He got up, rebuked the wind and said to the waves, "Quiet! Be still!" Then the wind died down and it was completely calm. (Mark 4:39)

He transformed the sin-ruined homes and habitations from places of devastation, desolation, and despair into beautiful, fertile, fruitful places where, under His wise rule, the oppressor is punished and the oppressed are lifted.

He has sent me to release the oppressed...
- Jesus reading the scroll of the prophet Isaiah in Nazareth (Luke 4:18)

Note: as the Almighty God performs miracle after miracle, "The upright see and rejoice, but all the wicked shut their mouths" (v. 42).

And thus the psalmist rightly declares: *Whoever is wise let him heed these things and consider the great love of the Lord* (v. 43).

Prayer:
Father, thank You for sending Jesus to release us from the strong bondage of sin, to heal and restore us, to release us from oppression. In Your presence, the storm is stilled to a whisper and all is calm. Your presence changes everything. You have come!

Psalm 108: When We Forget to Remember

Focus Verse:	New Testament Verse:
I will praise You, O LORD, among the nations; I will sing of you among the peoples. (3)	for it is God who works in you to will and to act according to his good purpose.
	Philippians 2:13

In this beautiful Psalm, David borrows from two other songs he has written, Psalm 57 and Psalm 60. Verses 1-5 are also found in Psalm 57:7-11. Verses 6-13 are also found in Psalm 60:5-12. In this prayer, first of praise, then a plea for help for the nation as they face enemy threats, there is woven throughout a shimmering gold thread of steadfast faith in a God of:

❖ Great love, higher than the heavens
❖ Faithfulness reaching to the skies
❖ Glory covering the entire earth.

David recognizes that God, who is absolutely essential for their victory, has rejected them, no longer going out with their armies. Thus, the repeated declarations of praise and pleading, for David knows his God is a God who saves, helps, delivers, speaks, intervenes, leads, and gives victory.

I wonder if David and his men had started getting cocky, taking credit for their victories, forgetting to praise God among the nations, to sing His praise among the peoples. How easily we become complacent, self-sufficient, and proud. How gradual the forgetting to remember, the edging out of God's presence and power in our lives, until suddenly we come up short and realize we have wandered far away from the wise guidance and protection of our all-loving, faithful, and glorious God. Thus, the interwoven praise and pleading as we recognize anew our need for God.

We need transformation from:
- ❖ Apathy → Action
- ❖ Barrenness → Boldness
- ❖ Complacency → Commitment
- ❖ Defeat → Declaration
- ❖ Prayerlessness → Prayerfulness
- ❖ Rebellion → Repentance
- ❖ Selfishness → Servanthood
- ❖ Thanklessness → Thankfulness
- ❖ Timidity → Triumph

Prayer:
Father, may I always remember and never forget and never be ashamed to declare Your praises so all can hear. Make me a blessing today.

_____
_____
_____
_____
_____
_____
_____
_____

Psalm 109: A God of Justice

Focus Verse:	New Testament Verse:
For He stands at the right hand of the needy one, to save his life from those who condemn him. (31)	whatever you did for one of the least of these brothers of mine, you did for me. Matthew 25:40

This troubling, most severe of the imprecatory Psalms of David, begins and ends with David humbly seeking his God's help, when again he is in a situation of being falsely accused and maligned by wicked and deceitful men.

The middle section, verses 5-19, full of bitterness, hatred, cursing, and vindictiveness (extending even to the family of the accused), is uncharacteristic of David. Some Bible scholars, noting the shift in these verses from the plural to the singular in verses 5-19, then the shift back to plural in verse 20, suggest David is, in these between verses, quoting the words of the very enemies that are misusing him.

The shining truth and promise of this puzzling Psalm yet gleams brightly:

Our God is just.

    He hates injustice.

He will, in His way, and in His time deal decisively with injustice.

God hates when the poor and needy are wounded, and in fact, stands at the right hand of the needy one to save his life from those who condemn him (v. 31). The wicked who callously take advantage of the disadvantaged-whether poor, needy, orphaned, widowed, persecuted, or falsely imprisoned-would do well to remember they are mistreating Almighty God for, *Whatever you did for one of the least of these brothers of mine, you did for me* (Matt. 25:40).

Prayer:
Father, show me opportunities when I can, through Your presence in my life, stand at the side of one who is poor, needy, or wounded.

Psalm 110: Who He Is

Focus Verse:	New Testament Verse:
The LORD says to my Lord: "Sit at my right hand until I make your enemies a footstool for your feet." (1)	"Therefore, let all Israel be assured of this: God has made this Jesus, whom you crucified both Lord and Christ."
	Acts 2:36

This is an amazing Messianic prophetic recording from the psalmist king who lived and reigned fourteen generations *before* Christ, the Messiah, came.

Here is the selected verse again with the pronouns named for clarification:

The Lord (Jehovah) *says to my* (David's) *Lord* (Jesus Christ): *"Sit at my* (Jehovah's) *right hand until I* (Jehovah) *make your* (Jesus') *enemies a footstool for your (Jesus') feet.*

Jesus Himself challenged the Pharisees, "Whose Son is Christ?" quoting these very words (Matt. 22:42-46 and again in Mark and Luke), leaving no room for doubt regarding the prophetic nature of this Psalm. In fact, this Psalm lays out the mission of the very Son of God. Though there will be a time of waiting-"until I make your enemies your footstool"-even now:

He is King. Jesus reigns in majesty at the right hand of God, *now*!

He is Priest. Jesus, from His position of authority, serves as our perfect High Priest-*forever* the source of eternal salvation.

*And once made perfect, He became the source of eternal salva-
tion for all who obey Him, and was designated by God to be
high priest in the order of Melchizedek.* (Heb. 5:9-10)

He is Judge. Jesus, when the day of His wrath-the day of battle-arrives, will once and for all crush and destroy all evil and all wickedness as He judges the nations. The psalmist poetically and beautifully describes God's own people willingly joining in the battle "as the dew rise from the womb of the night."

At that time there will be no doubt who Jesus is:

As Peter declared to the crowd at Pentecost, *Therefore, let all Israel be assured of this: God has made this Jesus, whom you crucified both Lord and Christ* (Acts 2:36).

Prayer:
Jesus, You are my King, my Priest, my Judge. You are both Lord and Christ.

_____
_____
_____
_____
_____
_____
_____
_____

Psalm 111: Wise Steps

Focus Verse:	New Testament Verse:
The fear of the LORD is the beginning of wisdom; all who follow his precepts have good understanding. To him belongs eternal praise. (10)	Since we live by the Spirit let us keep in step with the Spirit. Galatians 5:25

To Him belongs eternal praise for:
- ❖ His works are great (v. 2) and His deeds glorious and majestic (v. 3)
- ❖ His righteousness endures forever
- ❖ He brings His ways to our remembrance
- ❖ He is gracious and compassionate (v. 4)
- ❖ He provides our daily bread and keeps His promises (v. 5)
- ❖ He displays His powerful works through gaining victories on our behalf (v. 6)

"Thy kingdom come, Thy will be done..."
- ❖ He works on our behalf in faithfulness and justice (v. 7)
- ❖ His precepts are trustworthy and eternally steadfast (v. 8)
- ❖ He provided redemption, ordering His covenant forever (the way devised) (v. 9)
- ❖ Holy and awesome is His name.

Thus, in the heart considering all of this springs up a deep desire to fear the Lord, to walk in the light of His commands, to let His presence so permeate our lives that we increasingly reflect His glory, our daily lives a living sacrifice of overflowing praise.

This is true worship. This is wisdom.

Prayer:
Father, might I keep in step with You, my life a source of eternal praise.

Psalm 112: Increasingly Reflecting His Glory

Focus Verse:	New Testament Verse:
Blessed is the man who fears the LORD, who finds great delight in his commands (1)	And we, who with unveiled faces all reflect the Lord's glory, are being transformed into his likeness with ever increasing glory which comes from the Lord, who is the Spirit.
	2 Corinthians 3:18

The blessed man of verse 1 is the true praise-er of the proceeding Psalm, who, in his deepening appreciation of the greatness of his God, delights in His commands, strives to imitate Him (to follow hard after Him) and all the while is steadily, silently (almost imperceptibly) growing in wisdom (11:10).

- ❖ His home and family are blessed
- ❖ He is gracious, compassionate, generous, righteous, and just
- ❖ He is steadfast, unmoved by bad news, perilous times, and dark days, *for even in darkness light dawns for the upright* (v. 4)
- ❖ And the ultimate clincher: He is despised by the wicked!

This blessed man, this true praise-er is revealed to b an imitator of God. He is God's workmanship.

And we who with unveiled faces all reflect the Lord's glory, are being transformed into His likeness with ever increasing glory which comes from the Lord, who is the Spirit.
(2 Cor. 3:18)

Prayer:
Father, I want to increasingly reflect Your glory. The world badly needs the light of Your presence. I want to look more like Jesus and less like me, even though it means many will despise me.

Psalm 113: Stooping Down to Earth

Focus Verse:	New Testament Verse:
Who is like the LORD our God, the One who sits enthroned on high, who stoops down to look on the heavens and the earth? (5, 6)	Who being in very nature God, did not consider equality with God something to be grasped, but made himself nothing, taking the very nature of a servant, being made in human likeness. And being found in appearance as a man, he humbled himself and became obedient to death–even death on a cross. Philippians 2:6-8

Psalm 113 is the first of six Psalms (113-118) making up the Great Hallel, sung at Passover, Pentecost, and the Feast of Tabernacles. Thus it is highly likely that Jesus would have sung this hymn with His disciples in the Upper Room as they celebrated Passover together, hours before His arrest, trial, and crucifixion.

In the first part, the psalmist praised the exalted Lord, Jehovah, enthroned above, who, in lavish grace, stooped to look upon the earth, and not just to look, but to raise the poor and lift the needy. Our Jehovah Lord indeed stooped down to make us great, becoming flesh to dwell among us.

Paul describes this in his letter to the Philippian Christians:

> *Who being in very nature God, did not consider equality with God something to be grasped, but made Himself nothing, taking the very nature of a servant, being made in human likeness. And being found in appearance as a man, He humbled Himself*

and became obedient to death–even death on a cross.
(Phil. 2:6-8)

It is remarkable to realize Jesus sang the words of this Psalm with His disciples, including the words of the selected verse, even as the ultimate depth of His stooping was almost upon Him, the breaking of His body and the pouring out of His blood on our behalf.

And He took bread, gave thanks and broke it, and gave it to them saying, "This is my body given for you; do this in remembrance of me." (Luke 22:19-20)

Prayer:
Father, thanks so much for stooping to such depths that we might be lifted up out of the ash heap of our sinfulness to be seated with You on high. Thank You, that You who knew no sin became sin for us that we might become righteous.

Psalm 114: Birthing Christianity

Focus Verse:	New Testament Verse:
Tremble, O earth, at the presence of the Lord; at the presence of the God of Jacob, (7)	"I have told you these things, so that in me you may have peace. In this world you will have trouble. But take heart! I have overcome the world."
	John 16:33

In this the second of the six Psalms of the Great Hallel, the theme is of the Exodus (Exodus 12), including the dramatic crossing of the Red Sea (Exodus 14) and the later miraculous piling up in a heap of the swollen, flood-stage Jordan River, allowing the entire nation to cross over-*on dry land*-into the Promised Land (Joshua 3).

These events surround the first Passover, and thus as the mountains skipped like rams, the hills like lambs, and the earth trembled, a new nation was being born in the presence of the Lord Adon, the Sovereign Lord, of Eloah, the Mighty One.

Years later, as Jesus sang this hymn with His disciples in the Upper Room, He told them of the convulsions and agony they would face in their role in "birthing Christianity" (John 16:17-33). He prayed for them and even for us that evening for protection from evil as we live for Him in a hostile world (John 17).

The next day on the cross, as He declared "It is finished" and gave up His spirit, the earth shook and grew dark as the curtain in the temple separating the Holy Place from the Most Holy Place was torn in two from top to bottom, thus ushering in the New Covenant (Matt. 27:51).

In the last days, the earth will again tremble as all eyes see the Son of Man coming in the clouds of the sky, with power and great glory (Matt. 24:30).

Prayer:
Father, thank You for miraculously delivering us from sin. Give us the courage to stand for You in these last days. Though we know in this world we will have trouble, may we be encouraged and at peace, knowing You have overcome the world (John 16:33).

Psalm 115: The One and Only

Focus Verse:	New Testament Verse:
Not to us, O LORD, not to us but to your name be the glory, because of your love and faithfulness. (1)	No one has ever seen God, but God the One and Only, who is at the Father's side, has made him known.
	John 1:18

When they had sung a hymn, they went out to the Mount of Olives. (Matt. 26:30)

This, the third of the six Psalms of the Great Hallel, along with the fourth, fifth, and sixth, were most certainly verses in the hymn Jesus sang with His disciples after the Passover Feast and right before they went out to the Mount of Olives.

The nations ask, "Where is their God?" (v. 2)

In stark contrast to the handmade idols of silver and gold, who, in spite of having mouths, eyes, ears, noses, hands, feet, and throats, could not speak, see, hear, smell, feel, walk, or utter a sound, the all-powerful God became flesh, was even then standing among the disciples, leading them in this hymn of praise. He was about to offer the ultimate gift of life and faithfulness by dying on the cross to pay the price for the sinfulness of mankind.

No one has ever seen God, but God the One and Only, who is at the Father's side, has made Him known. (John 1:18)

The one who made God known now sang this hymn. How beautifully intertwined is this Psalm with John 1:1-18, and both should be read together.

Prayer:
Father, thank You for making Yourself known to us through Your Son, Jesus Christ, who has triumphed over sin and death and is even now at Your right hand in heaven.

Psalm 116: A Cup of Commitment

Focus Verse:	New Testament Verse:
I will lift up the cup of salvation and call on the name of the LORD. (13)	Then he took the cup, gave thanks and offered it to them saying, "Drink from it all of you. This is my blood of the covenant which is poured out for many for the forgiveness of sins. Matthew 26:27, 28

In this the fourth of the Psalms of the Great Hallel, the psalmist, having been delivered from deep trouble, sorrow, and anguish, asks, *How can I repay the Lord for all His goodness to me?* (v. 12).

The answer is immediately given, *I will lift up the cup of salvation and call on the name of the Lord* (v. 13).

It is a cup of commitment.

Earlier that evening, during what became known as the Last Supper, just before singing this verse of the Great Hallel with His disciples, Jesus took the cup, gave thanks, and offered it to them, saying: *Drink from it all of you. This is my blood of the covenant which is poured out for many for the forgiveness of sins* (Matt. 24:27-28; Mark 14:24; Luke 22:17-18, 20).

For our Savior, it was a cup of pain, sorrow, bitterness, unimaginable suffering, and being utterly forsaken. Hours later, in the Garden of Gethsemane, overwhelmed by sorrow and sweating drops of blood, Jesus pleaded with His Father, *If it is possible, may this cup be taken from Me. Yet not as I will but as You will* (Matt. 24:39).

Jesus ultimately drank that cup of bitterness on our behalf so the cup might become a cup of salvation, forgiveness, redemption, restoration, and blessing. As we lift that cup in remembrance and praise, we consider anew the price He paid.

Prayer:
Thank You, Jesus, for the overflowing cup of salvation. I lift it up in commitment to You.

Psalm 117: A Cup of Salvation

Focus Verse:	New Testament Verse:
For great is his love toward us, and the faithfulness of the LORD endures forever. Praise the LORD. (2)	But we have this treasure in jars of clay to show that this all-surpassing power is from God and not from us. 2 Corinthians 4:7

This short song of praise is for all nations and for all peoples, for His great love and His faithfulness extend to every nation, tribe, people, and language. The apostle John had a foretaste of this in his vision recorded in the book of Revelation 7:9-10: *Before me was a great multitude that no one could count, from every nation, tribe, people, and language, standing before the throne and in front of the Lamb... And they cried out in a loud voice, "Salvation belongs to our God, who sits on the throne and to the Lamb."*

It is these that have held up empty, cracked vessels of clay that His abundant love and faithfulness might be poured into broken, sin-shattered lives-the cup of salvation-full of grace and truth.

This fifth of the six Psalms of the Great Hallel returns to the theme of the third, that of the love and faithfulness of the Word became flesh. It is those of this multitude-spoken of in Revelation, beholding His glory full of grace and truth-who then offer their lives as living sacrifices of praise, sharing in His suffering, becoming like Him in His death, and so, somehow to attain to the resurrection from the dead. This is the great story of redemption.

For this, we, in spirit and in truth, worship, crying out in a loud voice along with the multitude:

Prayer:
Salvation belongs to our God, who sits on the throne and to the Lamb. Praise the Lord.

Psalm 118: His Light Shines Upon Us

Focus Verse:	New Testament Verse:
The LORD is God, and he has made his light shine upon us. (27)	"I am the light of the world. Whoever follows me will never walk in darkness, but will have the light of life." John 8:12

This last of the six Psalms of the Great Hallel is prophetic of the Messiah. Even as Jesus sang this hymn with His disciples at that last Passover together, it was being fulfilled before them. *I will not die but live, and will proclaim what the Lord has done. The Lord has chastened me severely, but He has not given me over to death* (vv. 17-18).
"I am the resurrection and the life." (John 11:25)
This is the gate of the Lord through which the righteous may enter (v. 20).
"I am the Way, the Truth, and the Life. No man comes to the Father except through Me." (John 14:6)
You have become my salvation (v. 21).
"Salvation is found in no one else, for there is no other name under heaven given to men by which we must be saved." (Acts 4:12)
The stone the builders rejected has become the capstone (v. 22).
"Then know this, you and all the people of Israel: It is by the name of Jesus Christ of Nazareth, whom you crucified but whom God raised from the dead, that this man stands before you healed. He is 'the stone you builders rejected, which has become the capstone.'" (Acts 4:10-11)
"For in scripture it says, 'See, I lay a stone in Zion, a chosen and precious cornerstone, and the one who trusts in Him will never be put to shame.' Now to you who believe, this

stone is precious. But to those who do not believe, 'The stone the builders rejected has become the capstone.'" (2 Pet. 4:6-7)

Blessed is He who comes in the name of the Lord (v. 26).

"The next day John saw Jesus coming toward him and said, 'Look, the Lamb of God, who takes away the sin of the world!'" (John 1:29)

"For I tell you, you will not see me again until you say, 'Blessed is He who comes in the name of the Lord.'" (Matt. 24:39)

The Lord is God and He has made His light shine upon us (v. 27).

"I am the light of the world." (John 8:12)

As the last strains of the hymn were sung, Jesus went out into the night to face His agony in the garden, His arrest, and His crucifixion, that He might bring about the ultimate fulfillment of the Passover as the once and for all sacrificial Lamb, the ultimate Exodus: the deliverance from sin.

Thus we offer this Psalm's refrain in gratitude as our prayer.

Prayer:
Your love endures forever.

Psalm 119: The God-breathed Word

Focus Verse:	New Testament Verse:
The law from your mouth is more precious to me than thousands of pieces of silver and gold. (72)	All Scripture is God-breathed and is useful for teaching, rebuking, correcting and training in righteousness, so that the man of God may be thoroughly equipped for every good work. 2 Timothy 3:16, 17

Blessed are they whose ways are blameless, who walk according to the law of the Lord (v. 1).

The opening verse of the magnificent Psalm lays out the theme flowing throughout each of the twenty-two carefully composed sections, that of praise for the Word of God. This Psalm, the longest of all the Psalms, and the longest chapter in the Bible, is an acrostic, with each of its twenty-two sections, one for each letter of the Hebrew alphabet, having eight verses each, all beginning with the letter of the section. This Psalm is located at the exact center of the Bible, just as God's Word should be central to our lives.

Our selected verse is located in the *Teth* section of the Psalm.

In *Teth* and *Yah*, we learn about the blessings of affliction. I can say with the psalmist in fullest sincerity:

Before I was afflicted, I went astray, but now I obey Your word (v. 67).

It was good for me to be afflicted so that I might learn Your decrees (v. 71).
I know, O Lord, that Your laws are righteous and in faithfulness You have afflicted me (v. 75).

Until emerging from the crucible of affliction, one realizes: *The law from Your mouth is more precious to me than thousands of pieces of silver and gold* (v. 72).
How poignant the ending verse of this brilliant Psalm and it is our prayer:

Prayer:
I have strayed like a lost sheep. Seek Your servant, for I have not forgotten Your commands (v. 176).

Psalm 120 A song of ascents (Psalms 120-134): Strangers on Earth

Focus Verse:	New Testament Verse:
I will call on the LORD in my distress, and he answers me. (1)	And they admitted that they were aliens and strangers on earth.
	Instead, they were longing for a better country—a heavenly one. Therefore God is not ashamed to be called their God, for He prepared a city for them.
	Hebrews 11:13, 16

This Psalm is the first of the fifteen Psalms labeled as "A song of ascents," all centered on the City of God and the Temple. In the first, the psalmist, far from this city, cries out in distress, troubled by the lies, deceitfulness, and violence of those he lives among. This brings to mind verses from the great faith chapter in Hebrews describing the mindset of the heroes of the faith:

And they admitted that they were aliens and strangers on earth... instead they were longing for a better country, — a heavenly one. Therefore God is not ashamed to be called their God, for He prepared a city for them (Heb. 11:13-16).

For we are not of this world.

Prayer:
Father, increasingly, I feel like a stranger here on Earth. I too cry out in distress as I experience all the lying, deceit, and discord swirling around me. I am so grateful that You hear our prayers and that You answer them. Jesus specifically prayed for me and all of my fellow believers that last evening of His earthly life, for He knew firsthand

the struggles we would experience. You have perfectly equipped us to participate in Your divine nature, bringing about Your kingdom on Earth as it is in heaven, even *today*, even *now*. While we groan and long for deliverance, it is right and good that we are not contented here.

Psalm 121: Pressing On

Focus Verse:	New Testament Verse:
I lift up my eyes to the hills–where does my help come from? My help comes from the LORD, the Maker of heaven and earth. (1, 2)	Forgetting what is behind and straining toward what is ahead, I press on toward the goal to win the prize for which God has called me heavenward in Christ Jesus. Philippians 3:13b, 14

In this, the second song of ascents, one can imagine a traveling pilgrim on his way to Jerusalem, just beginning to glimpse the hills of Jerusalem in the distance as he approached the end of his sojourn.

The pilgrim yet recognizes that as much as he longs for the city and his temple, the Lord his maker is and ever has been with him at his side, continually watching over him, even through the night, on through the day, ever at his right side, keeping the faithful pilgrim from all harm and evil, watching over his coming and going both now and forevermore. The pilgrim may have in that moment of mingled glimpsing and longing recalled the precious words of the law, *but if from there* (Deut. 4:29).

Did he ponder the repeated failures and returning of his people, his personal relationship with his God? Did he express longing for the promised Messiah? Nevertheless, the Lord, ever vigilant, watches over you. It is enough.

Prayer:
Father, thank You, the Maker of heaven and Earth, that You are ever by my side daily, providing the help I need as I press on heavenward.

Psalm 122: He Dwells With Us

Focus Verse:	New Testament Verse:
I rejoiced with those who said to me, "Let us go to the house of the LORD." (1)	I saw the Holy City, the new Jerusalem, coming down out of heaven from God, prepared as a bride beautifully dressed for her husband. And I heard a loud voice from the throne saying, "Now the dwelling of God is with men, and He will live with them. They will be His people, and God Himself will be with them and be their God.
	Revelation 21:2, 3

Pray for the peace of Jerusalem: "May those who love you be secure..."

In this the third of the song of ascents, our singer has now arrived at the city and the longed-for house of the LORD. He rejoices at the opportunity to worship at the very house of the Lord and to stand in the very gate of this great city of the King of the earth, on which all spiritual life centers.

The singer prays for the peace and prosperity of this great city, for what this city will one day truly be, "the embodiment of the ideals of God for his people, the realization on their part of the order of peace and prosperity which is His will for them" (Morgan, 1994).

Today, we yet live by faith and not by sight. Jerusalem is far from peace, though still we pray for this peace for all peoples. We see through the present earthly chaos to the great shining future. With John, we envision *the Holy City, the new Jerusalem, coming down out of heaven from God, prepared as a bride beautifully dressed for her husband. And I heard a loud voice say, "Now the dwelling of God is with men, and He will live with them and be their God"* (Rev. 21:2-3).

Prayer:
Father, how we long for the new Jerusalem. Yet even now, through your Holy Spirit, you dwell with us. Bring your peace to our lives.

_____
_____
_____
_____
_____
_____
_____
_____

Psalm 123: Fixing Our Eyes

Focus Verse:	New Testament Verse:
I lift up my eyes to you; to you whose throne is in heaven. As the eyes of slaves look to the hand of their master, as the eyes of a maid look to the hand of her mistress, so our eyes look to the LORD our God, till he shows us His mercy. (1, 2)	Let us fix our eyes on Jesus, the author and perfecter of our faith, who for the joy set before him endured the cross, scorning its shame, and sat down at the right hand of the throne of God. Hebrews 12:2

How beautiful this is. Our singer, having entered the city gates and entering the temple, now approaches the throne. How beautiful this attitude of complete submission in service, of utter dependence for mercy and rescue from difficult circumstances. This intimate relationship of being perfectly attuned to the wishes and ways of the Master so that by the vigilant watching of the Master's hand, the servant responds in perfect obedience to the slightest movement.

Am I that:
- ❖ Focused
- ❖ Submissive
- ❖ Dependent
- ❖ Attuned
- ❖ Attentive

Prayer:
Father, thank You, that through the work of Jesus Christ, I can approach the throne of grace with confidence to receive mercy and find grace. Help me to fix my eyes

on Jesus so I will be perfectly attuned to Your will and Your ways.

Psalm 124: Our Helper

Focus Verse:	New Testament Verse:
Our help is in the name of the LORD, the Maker of heaven and earth. (8)	So we say with confidence, "The Lord is my helper; I will not be afraid. What can man do to me?"
	Hebrews 13:6

How extraordinary to realize, to stop and ponder, that the divine Creator and Sustainer of all things personally comes to my aid.

As did the writer of Hebrews, we can confidently declare, "The Lord is my helper; I will not be afraid. What can man do to me?" He promises to never leave us nor forsake us. If the Lord had not been with him, the singer shares:

- ❖ The attackers would have swallowed us alive
- ❖ The floods engulfed us
- ❖ The torrents swept over us
- ❖ We would have been torn by their teeth.

Instead, it was as if he had escaped the fowler's snare. What an apt illustration of what Peter later described as "allowing us to escape the corruption caused by evil desires." This ultimate rescue is the rescue from sin and death.

"Fear not, for I have redeemed you," the prophet Isaiah said, speaking of the Messiah (Isaiah 43:1), so that even when passing through waters and rivers, they will not sweep over you; and when walking through the fires, you will not be burned.

Prayer:
Thank You, Father, for Your perfect provision, protection, and plan.

Psalm 125: Surrounded By His Protection

Focus Verse:	New Testament Verse:
The scepter of the wicked will not remain over the land allotted to the righteous, for then the righteous might use their hands to do evil. (3)	What, then, shall we say in response to this? If God is for us, who can be against us? He who did not spare His own Son, but gave Him up for us all–how will He not graciously give us all things?–Romans 8:31, 32

One can imagine the singer pilgrim as he approached Jerusalem, considering the mountains as they came into view, protectively surrounding the Holy City and thinking, as he sings this song of ascents, what a beautiful picture the mountains are of the way our God surrounds us with His love, mercy, and protection.

Daily trusting in the enduring protection of the Lord ever surrounding us.

Never compromising or conforming.

Unshakeable like Mount Zion.

Ever steadfastly about our Father's business, doing our part as He lives through us, ushering in, "Thy kingdom come, Thy will be done, on earth as it is in heaven."

    For indeed, "This is my Father's world."

The scepter of the wicked will not remain over the land allotted to the righteous...

    "For though the wrong seems oft so strong, He is the Ruler yet."

For if God is for us, who can be against us?

Janice Stauffer MacLeod

Prayer:
Father, as Jesus prayed for all believers of all times on the night of His betrayal, "Protect them from the evil one," lead us not into temptation but deliver us from evil. For Thine is the kingdom and the power and the glory *now* and forever and ever. Amen.

Psalm 126: Sowing Seed

Focus Verse:	New Testament Verse:
He who goes out weeping carrying seed to sow, will return with songs of joy, carrying sheaves with him. (6)	Let us not become weary in doing good, for at the proper time we will reap a harvest if we do not give up.
	Galatians 6:9

The singer opens his song recalling the overwhelming joy of being restored to Zion, noting how even the surrounding nations remarked about the great things the Lord had done for them. But then the singer pleads that his people may more fully realize and take hold of that which God has and will continue to restore to them, possessing that which they have been given to possess.

"Like streams in the Negev," the psalmist sings (v. 4).

The Negev was a dry, barren stretch of land south of Judah where, in the summer months, the streams dried up completely. The singer here envisions his people's full restoration to the joys and blessings of the Lord, just as these empty stream beds were once again filled with the autumn rains. Thus this perpetual prayer, "Restore us again, Lord," that we might, in spite of the most arid conditions, receive a harvest of joy, having faithfully carried forth the seed to sow.

Is the seed to be sown, first of all our prayers, our faithful continued prayers even during times of barrenness in our own lives or in the lives of our local church, or among the extended body of believers?

Is it also our steadfast abiding in the vine of the Word, our faithful living out of the Word by both example and by declaration? Is it standing on His promises and refusing to let go until He blesses us?

"Let us not become weary in doing good," the apostle Paul encouraged the Galatians, "for at the proper time we will reap a harvest if we do not give up" (Gal. 6:9).

Prayer:
Father, help us to faithfully sow in word and deed in such a way as to please the Spirit, thus reaping eternal life.

Psalm 127: God-built

Focus Verse:	New Testament Verse:
Unless the LORD builds the house, its builders labor in vain. Unless the LORD watches over the city, the watchmen stand guard in vain. (1)	Therefore, everyone who hears these words of mine and puts them into practice is like a wise man who builds his house on the rock. The rain came down, the streams rose, and the winds blew and beat against that house; yet it did not fall, because it had its foundation on the rock.
	Matthew 7:24, 25

The seed of faith takes root and sprouts in the individual heart then extends to the home, and then into our churches, our communities, and into the uttermost parts of the world.

How important that we each attend to our own section of the wall, building or repairing it accordingly, doing what we can, where we are, so through Christ living in us, we do our part to usher in Thy kingdom come, Thy will be done (even here and now) as it is in heaven. Personal repentance, family repentance, church and corporate repentance, national repentance, global repentance. Setting ourselves to heart rending versus garment rending.

"As for me and my house, we will serve the Lord," Joshua declared without hesitation as he inherited the mantle of leadership from Moses. We each face the same decision today and the choice we make has eternal repercussions.

Prayer:

Father, bless each room in our home, every meal that is shared, all our conversation, every visitor that crosses our threshold, all of our hopes, dreams, and plans. May Your name be truly honored and hallowed here such that it is noticed when guests enter. Remind us to always obey Your precepts. May we, like Timothy, continue in what we have learned and become convinced of, having known from infancy the holy scriptures, which are able to make us wise for salvation through Jesus Christ. May our homes be built on the rock-solid foundation of Your Word so no matter the severity of the storms or the intensity of the tumult in the world we live in, our house will not fall down.

Father, I am so grateful for my godly heritage. May we faithfully pass it on to the next generation.

_____
_____
_____
_____
_____
_____
_____
_____

Psalm 128: Walking in His Ways

Focus Verse:	New Testament Verse:
Blessed are all who fear the LORD, who walk in his ways. (1)	I have come that they may have life, and have it to the full. John 10:10b

Those who walk in His ways daily experience the blessing of fruitful, fulfilled, peaceful lives, godly families, and stable homes. Living a life ordered by the very Author of life leads to blessing and prosperity. That does not mean there are not trials, temptations, and tempests. It means, with God's guidance, the devoted follower steadfastly stays the course, knowing God is ever steadily working out His purpose.

The follower-after the ways of God becomes an oasis in a barren place, a beautiful well-watered garden in a sun-scorched land, a tree planted by the rivers of water, a spring whose waters never fail, a bright light in a dark place. Life as God intended. The family blessed by God, dwelling in the house built by God, inhabiting the city guarded by God.

As we witness the rapid unraveling of family life and moral underpinnings in our nation and our world today, may we who know You, Your Word, and Your ways, commit ourselves wholeheartedly to walking in Your ways, regardless of the cost. Jesus came that we may have life, and have it to the fullest. Jesus is the Way. Jesus is the Truth. Jesus is the Life. No man comes to the Father but through Jesus.

How badly our world needs us to be blameless and pure, children of God, without fault in a crooked and depraved generation, shining like stars as we hold out the word of life (Phil. 2:15-16).

Prayer:
Father, recognizing that the time is short, may we, without shame, fear, or timidity, as Paul instructed the young Timothy, "Preach the Word; be prepared in season and out of season; correct, rebuke and encourage-with great patience and careful instruction" (2 Tim. 4:2-3).

Psalm 129: The Only Way

Focus Verse:	New Testament Verse:
May all who hate Zion be turned back in shame. (5)	Enter through the narrow gate. For wide is the gate and broad is the road that leads to destruction, and many enter through it. But small is the gate and narrow the road that leads to life, and only a few find it.
	Matthew 7:13, 14

In this song of ascents and pilgrimage, the singer recalls the continual great oppression of his people since his youth and before. The oppressors have not yet gained the victory! Nor will they ever, for the Lord has cut His people free from the cords of the wicked oppressors. The Lord of deliverance will ultimately bring to shame all those who hate Zion.

As persecution against believers in God increases around the globe, as even here in this nation founded under God, He is edged out of every aspect of our lives, we believers remaining, as did the singer, yet rejoice in our ultimate deliverance from and God's total triumph over evil.

All who hate Zion, all who hate the Messiah-the Way, the Truth, and the Life-all who dishonor God, our great deliverer, will one day be turned back in shame.

In the Gospel of Matthew, Jesus tells the parable of the sheep and the goats in which He describes the turning back of all those (the goats) who rejected Him.

> Depart from me, you who are cursed, into the eternal fire prepared for the devil and his angels. For I was hungry and you gave me nothing to

eat, I was thirsty, and you gave me nothing to drink, I was a stranger and you did not invite me in, I needed clothes and you did not clothe me, I was sick and in prison and you did not look after me. (Matt. 25:41-43)

One day, every eye will see Him. One day all will stand before Him. One day all will be separated into two groups. Those that honored Him and those that rejected Him. Those that found and pursued the narrow way of life, and those that, without thought, ran pell-mell down the wide way that leads to death and destruction.

Prayer:
Father, thank You for sending Jesus to be the Way, the Truth, and the Life. Thank You that He, through His death and resurrection, has triumphed over sin and death. Thank You that He is my Savior.

Psalm 130 (A Penitential Psalm, A Paulini Psalm): The Roman Road

Focus Verse:	New Testament Verse:
Out of the depths I cry to You, O LORD; (1)	For the wages of sin is death, but the gift of God is eternal life in Christ Jesus our Lord.
	Romans 6:23

Martin Luther called this Psalm, along with Psalm 32, 51, 130, and 143 Paulini Psalms, as they recognize the need for forgiveness of sin without having any works of the law to offer.

This Psalm could also be called the Roman Road Psalm.

Out of the depths I cry to You, O Lord (v. 1).

"For all have sinned and fall short of the glory of God" (Rom. 3:23).

O Lord, hear my voice. Let Your ears be attentive to my cry for mercy (v. 2).

"For whosoever shall call upon the name of the Lord shall be saved" (Rom. 10:13).

If You, O Lord, kept a record of sins, O Lord, who could stand? (v. 3)

"For the wages of sin is death" (Rom. 6:23a).

But with You there is forgiveness, therefore You are feared (v. 4).

"Blessed are they whose transgressions are forgiven, whose sins are covered. Blessed is the man whose sin the Lord will never count against him." (Rom. 4:7-8)

I wait for the Lord, my soul waits, and in His word I put my hope (v. 5).

"But the gift of God is eternal life through Jesus Christ our Lord." (Rom. 6:23b)

My soul waits for the Lord more than the watchmen wait for the morning (v. 6).

> "For in this hope we were saved. But hope that is seen is no hope at all. Who hopes for what he already has? But if we hope for what we do not yet have, we wait for it patiently." (Rom. 8:24-25)

O Israel, put your hope in the Lord, for with the Lord is unfailing love (v. 7).

> "But God commendeth His love toward us, in that, while we were yet sinners, Christ died for us." (Rom. 5:8)

And with Him is full redemption (v. 7).

> "That if thou shalt confess with thy mouth the Lord Jesus, and shalt believe in thine heart that God hath raised Him from the dead, though shalt be saved." (Rom. 10:9)

With you:
- There is forgiveness (v. 4)   I am saved (salvation)
- There is unfailing love (v. 7)   I am being saved (sanctification)
- There is full redemption (v. 7)   I will be saved (glorification)

The sinner realizes his condition.
Upon realizing his condition, the sinner cries to the Lord for mercy.
Having cried to the Lord for mercy, the sinner receives forgiveness for all his sins.
Having received forgiveness, the believer begins to live a life of hope and watchfulness, progressively guided by the unfailing love of his Savior.

Since hope will not disappoint, the believer will ultimately receive full redemption as a child of the King in the heavenly kingdom.

Prayer:
Father, thank You that with You there is forgiveness. With You there is unfailing love. With You there is full redemption.

Psalm 131: Acceptance with Joy

Focus Verse:	New Testament Verse:
But I have stilled and quieted my soul; like a weaned child with its mother, like a weaned child is my soul within me. (2)	And the peace of God, which transcends all understanding, will guard your hearts and your minds in Christ Jesus. Philippians 4:7 I have learned the secret of being content in any and every situation, whether well fed or hungry, whether living in plenty or in want. I can do everything though Him who gives me strength. Philippian 4:12b, 13

This particular song of ascents is of David. David, Israel's greatest king, knew the value of humility. He rightly understood his position in relationship to his Almighty God.

Instead of pride, haughtiness, or obsession with self-importance, true children of God find themselves, as David described in this song, perfectly calm, content, and quiet in the presence of their Lord, for the very reason that He is with them. It is this spirit of satisfaction, contentment, and peace that transcends understanding, and leads to the steadfastness that is characteristic of God's own.

It is the acceptance with joy of God's will, knowing with certainty that He is working His purpose out for the good of those who love Him, even when the child of God cannot fathom what His is doing or how the puzzle pieces fit together to form a more beautiful whole. It is the realizing of God's perspective, that as the heavens are higher than the earth, so are His thoughts and ways higher than our own (Isa. 55:9). At this point in eternity,

His thoughts and His ways prove "too wonderful for me, too lofty for me to attain" (Ps. 139:7).

So though their view of God is imperfect and incomplete, the child of God, apprehending enough of God's character, not only puts their hope in the Lord, but is compelled to urge their fellow sojourners to this life of faith and surety as well.

Prayer:
Father, thank You, that in You I have all that I need, every good thing. Thank You for the gift of contentment, quietness, and peace.

Psalm 132: Urgently About His Business

Focus Verse:	New Testament Verse:
"I will not enter my house or go to my bed–I will allow no sleep to my eyes, no slumber to my eyelids, till I find a place for my LORD, a dwelling place for the Mighty One of Jacob." (3-5)	"wist ye not that I must be about my Father's business." Luke 2:49 (KJV)

The pilgrim singer in this song of ascents, likely written by King Solomon, sings of King David's lifelong heart's desire to build a temple, a dwelling place for his God. It was David's son, King Solomon, who built the temple, according to the plans and with the provisions his father David, through God's direction and leading, had left for him and instructed him to follow.

What if today we had a similar all-consuming passion to do all we could, through His Spirit, working in us to build His kingdom on Earth ("Thy kingdom come, Thy will be done on earth as it is in heaven")?

David's passion to build his God a temple for His dwelling place is recorded in 2 Sam. 7 and is good companion reading for this Psalm as we consider our own commitment to fulfill the Great Commission of our Lord. So too are the chapters in 1 Chron. 28-29, where David's God-directed plans and provisions for the temple are recorded.

The Plan:
The Spirit had put the plans in his mind for the courts... rooms... treasuries. . . divisions of priests and Levites... articles used in service... David states, "I have in writing

from the hand of the Lord upon me, and He gave me understanding in all the details of the plan" (1 Chron. 28:11-19).

The Provision:
"With all my resources I have provided for the temple of my God." (1 Chron. 29:1-9).

The Prayer:
"O Lord, our God, as for all this abundance that we have provided for building you a temple for your holy name, it comes from your hand, and all of it belongs to you. I know, my God, that you test the heart and are pleased with integrity. All these things have I given willingly and with honest intent. And now I have seen with joy how willingly your people who are here have given to you. O Lord, God of our fathers, keep this desire in the hearts of your people forever, and keep their hearts loyal to you. And give my son Solomon the wholehearted devotion to keep your commands, requirements, and decree, and to do everything to build the palatial structure for which I have provided" (1 Chron. 29:10-20).

Prayer:
Father, just as David prayed for his son Solomon, make us strong, courageous, and devoted to Your work of building Your kingdom on Earth. Help us to do Your work, of going into all the world to make disciples until it is finished and You return in all Your glory.

Psalm 133: Crushed Grapes

Focus Verse:	New Testament Verse:
How good and pleasant it is when brothers live together in unity! (1)	But even if I am being poured out like a drink offering on the sacrifice and service coming from your faith, I am glad and rejoice with all of you. Philippians 2:17

It is like a precious oil poured on the head (v. 2).

It is as if the dew of Hermon were falling on Mount Zion (v. 3).

It is first the consecrated life. The life set apart for service. Crushed grapes, broken bread, dying to self, that Christ might live through the one thus surrendered; the beautiful fragrance of His extravagant love filling the room; His footsteps of grace left behind wherever His servant passes.

For you have died, and your life is now hidden with Christ in God (Col. 3:3).

It is the fellowship of sharing in His sufferings, becoming like Him in His death (Phil. 3:10).

A life thus lived, fellowshipping with other lives thus ordered will then, as naturally as the dew falls uniformly over the land, bring peace and blessing and beauty; His blessing and beauty flowing from us; bringing refreshment in a parched land. How badly our barren Earth needs the blessings and beauty of such surrendered lives today.

"And so somehow to attain to the resurrection of the dead" (Phil. 3:11).

"But even if I am being poured out like a drink offering on the sacrifice and service coming from your faith, I am glad and rejoice with all of you" (Phil. 2:17).
Therefore, as God's chosen people, holy and dearly loved, clothe yourselves with compassion ... And over all these virtues put on love, which binds them all together in perfect unity (Col. 3:12-14).

Prayer:
Father, help me daily die to self that Christ may live through me.

Psalm 134: Perpetual Praise

Focus Verse:	New Testament Verse:
Praise the LORD all you servants of the LORD who minister by night in the house of the LORD. (1)	I want men everywhere to lift up holy hands in prayer, without anger or disputing. 1 Timothy 2:8

This is the final of the fifteen songs of ascent (of pilgrimage). In its brief three verses, it is yet a beautiful picture of the church, the body of Christ. Those servants minister by night, representing those who for the sake of their daily duties cannot be there, in a circle of perpetual praise and blessing. This picture can be extended to the church at large to all the corners of the globe. Is there ever a minute of the day or night when a believer is not murmuring the "Our Father"?

How beautiful I have often thought is this triangle of prayer uniting believers and loved ones all over the world as we each pray and praise our Father who art in heaven. Consider the selected verse from the previous song of ascent: *How good and pleasant it is when brothers live together in unity* (Ps. 133:1).

For how can believers not be united in spite of differences as we bow down and worship the Almighty, the Creator and Sustainer of all things, Our Father who art in heaven? Paul instructed the young Timothy, "I want men everywhere to lift up holy hands in prayer without anger or disputing" (1 Tim. 2:8)

Prayer:
Oh Father, teach us the gift of unceasing, united prayer and praise.

Psalm 135: Becoming Like What We Worship

Focus Verse:	New Testament Verse:
Those who make them will be like them, and so will all who trust in them. (18)	As for you, you were dead in your transgressions and sins, in which you used to live when you followed the ways of this world and of the ruler of the kingdom of the air, the spirit who is now at work in those who are disobedient.
	But because of His great love for us, God, who is rich in mercy, made us alive with Christ even when we were dead in transgressions–it is by grace you have been saved.
	Ephesians 2:1, 2, 4, 5

Those who make idols and put their trust in them will be like them: impotent in every way:

- ❖ With mouths but unable to speak or breathe
- ❖ With eyes but unable to see
- ❖ With ears but unable to hear

They are in fact dead. Dead in their trespasses and sin (Eph. 2:1).

In contrast: "Because of His great love for us, God who is rich in mercy, made us alive with Christ, even when we were dead in transgressions-it is by grace you have been saved" (Eph. 2:5).

We are created in the image of our Creator. We are made to praise and bring glory to our God as we live a life overflowing in worship to the one true God. As we live such a life, we increasingly reflect the Lord's glory as we are

Janice Stauffer MacLeod | 283

transformed into His likeness with ever increasing glory (2 Cor. 3:18).
We become like Him. We become like whom we worship.

Prayer:
Father, I would like to be like Jesus.

Psalm 136: Extravagant Love

Focus Verse:	New Testament Verse:
His love endures forever. (1-26)	God has poured out his love into our hearts by the Holy Spirit, whom he has given us.
	Romans 5:5b

Give thanks to the Lord for:
- ❖ He is good

His love endures forever.
- ❖ He is the One and only Almighty God

His love endures forever.
- ❖ He is the Creator and Sustainer of all things

His love endures forever.
- ❖ He is the great Deliverer

His love endures forever.
- ❖ He is our Guide, our Protector, our Defender

His love endures forever.
- ❖ He remembers us

His love endures forever.
- ❖ He frees us

His love endures forever.
- ❖ He is our Provider (our daily bread)

His love endures forever.

Reflecting on who our God is, His character, His works on our-the children of God-behalf, thus out of a heart overflowing with gratitude, gives thanks to the Lord.

Prayer:
Father, in a constantly shifting world where nothing can be depended upon, thank You that Your love endures forever.

Psalm 137: The Silent Song

Focus Verse:	New Testament Verse:
How can we sing songs of the LORD while in a foreign land? (4)	No, in all these things we are more than conquerors through him who loved us.
	Romans 8:37

With their city torn down to its foundations and banished to a strange land, it was too much to ask when their tormentors and captors demanded they sing songs of joy. The captive people of Israel, as one, hung their harps on the trees by the rivers of Babylon and sat down in silence. This poignant Psalm records the thoughts of the people, God's chosen ones, as they silently sat. Their "song of silence," unheard by their captors, was yet heard by their Jehovah God. It was a song or remembrance of their beloved city and their Lord.
George Campbell Morgan shares this illumination of this heart-wrenching Psalm:

> These great songs of the heart, finding no utterance for the ears of man, but expressing some of the deepest things of faith and life, constitute the inspirations which cleanse the soul, and generate the focus which at last breaks the bonds of captivity, and restores the people of God to the City of their love. (Morgan, 1994)

Ears begin to hear the unheard.
Eyes begin to focus on the unseen.
Tongues break forth in silent songs of praise.

Janice Stauffer MacLeod

This is a life lived in the secret place of the Most High, while all the time living physically in the darkest darkness, the deepest of depths, the most desperate desperation. More than a conqueror.

Prayer:
Oh, Father.

Psalm 138: Knowing God Up Close

Focus Verse:	New Testament Verse:
The LORD will fulfill His purposes for me; (8a) The LORD will perfect that which concerneth me. (8) (KJV)	Let us fix our eyes on Jesus, the author and perfecter of our faith, who for the joy set before him endured the cross, scorning its shame, and sat down at the right hand of the throne of God. Consider him who endured such opposition from sinful men, so that you will not grow weary and lose heart. Hebrews 12:2,3

This is another Psalm of David, the man after God's own heart, but yet who also experienced monumental failures. This was a man, as are all of us, who could in no way depend on his own abilities for this accomplishment, but instead understood completely that he must, could, and would depend entirely on his God for this perfecting work.

His God, our God of...
>Perfect holiness
>>Perfect love
>>>Perfect faithfulness

Who, though high and exalted, hears and comes near to those who call on Him.
In contrast, the proud He knows from afar.
He, the author and perfecter of our salvation, seeks to build an intimate relationship with us.

Janice Stauffer MacLeod

Prayer:
Father, I want to know You, up close and personal. I thank You that You give me everything I need for life and godliness.

Psalm 139: Seeing Our Hearts from God's Perspective

Focus Verse:	New Testament Verse:
O Lord, you have searched me and you know me. (1)	Nothing in all creation is hidden from God's sight. Everything is uncovered and laid bare before the eyes of him to who we must give account.
	Hebrews 4:13

You know:
When I sit
When I rise
My thoughts (even before I think them)
When I go out
When I lie down
The words I will speak

Your hand is always on me, surrounding and protecting me.
There is no place I can go to escape Your presence, no matter how high or low or near or far I go.
I can't even hide in the dark, for the light of Your presence overcomes the dark.
It was Your very hands that knit me together, that built my frame and wove my being into me.
You planned each of my days and wrote the story of my life even before I was conceived.
I am always in Your thoughts.
You know me better than I know myself and thus my prayer...

Janice Stauffer MacLeod

Prayer:
Search me, O God, and know my heart; test me and know my anxious thoughts. See if there is any offensive way in me and lead me in the way everlasting (vv. 23-24). Show me what You see when You look at me.

Psalm 140: Leaving Room for God's Wrath

Focus Verse:	New Testament Verse:
O Sovereign LORD, my strong deliver, who shields my head in the day of battle — (7)	Do not take revenge, my friends, but leave room for God's wrath, for it is written: "It is mine to avenge; I will repay," says the Lord. On the contrary: "If your enemy is hungry, feed him; if he is thirsty, give him something to drink. In doing this, you will heap burning coal on his head."
	Do not be overcome by evil, but overcome evil with good.
	Romans 12:19-21

This is another Psalm of David. It is the plea of a desperate heart, wrongly accused, slandered, tricked by evil, violent, devious, proud, wicked men. David of all people knew what it was like to be in these circumstances. He had plenty of experience in throwing himself upon his God seeking His:

- ❖ Rescue
- ❖ Protection (shielding)
- ❖ Deliverance

David knows full well and accepts that it is up to God to avenge, yet implores Him to seek that revenge even now to thwart the plans of the wicked.

While waiting for God to act (leaving room for God's wrath), the believer has been instructed on how to bring burning coals down on the (unprotected) heads of our enemies through our undeserved kindness to them (Rom.

12), while all the time experiencing God's shielding of our heads, protecting us from all wrong accusations, slander, tricks, and violence.

Prayer:
Father, You are a God of justice. We seek Your rescue, shielding, and deliverance. Help us to leave room for Your wrath. Help us to look for opportunities to do good to those who would bring us harm, thus allowing good to overcome evil.

_____
_____
_____
_____
_____
_____
_____
_____

Psalm 141: Recognizing Our Vulnerabilities

Focus Verse:	New Testament Verse:
let me not eat of their delicacies. (4b)	In the same way, count yourselves dead to sin but alive to God in Christ Jesus. Therefore do not let sin reign in your mortal body so that you obey its evil desires. Do not offer the parts of your body to sin, as instruments of wickedness, but rather offer yourselves to God as those who have been brought from death to life; and offer the parts of your body to him as instruments of righteousness. For sin shall not be your master, because you are not under law, but under grace. Romans 6:11-14

Here, the psalmist, David, in similar circumstances to the previous Psalm, again calls urgently to his Lord, for now the situation in his soul has grown more dangerous. Now David needs the protection only God can give from his tendency (and ours) to be "drawn to what is evil," "to take part in evil deeds with men who are evildoers," and "to eat of their delicacies."

Recognizing his vulnerability to this subtle change of tactics of his enemies, David pleads with God to:

Come quickly to me
  Hear my voice
    Set a guard over my mouth
      Keep watch over the door of my lips
        Nor let my heart be drawn to evil
          Keep me from the snares they have laid for me
            Protect me from the traps set by evildoers

David chooses to fix his eyes on this Sovereign Lord. David chooses to take refuge in Him.

It is a choice a believer has, through the power of Christ living within us, to put the brakes on sin (to not let sin reign) and as did David, offer our bodies as instruments of righteousness. At times like these, the believer should absolutely engulf the throne room of God with the incense of our prayers for protection, recognizing our struggle is not against flesh and blood, but against the rulers, against the authorities, against the powers of this dark world and against the spiritual forces in the heavenly realms. We are instructed to put on the full armor of God so that when the day of evil comes, we will be able to stand our ground (Eph. 6:10-13).

Prayer:

Father, help us, as You did for David, to recognize our vulnerability to sin. You have promised You will not let us be tempted beyond what we can bear, but will provide a way out so we can stand up under it (1 Cor. 10:12-13). Father, lead us not into temptation but deliver us from evil.

_____
_____
_____
_____
_____
_____
_____

Psalm 142: He Knows My Way

Focus Verse:	New Testament Verse:
When my spirit grows faint within me, it is you who knows my way. (3)	We are hard pressed on every side, but not crushed; perplexed, but not in despair; persecuted, but not abandoned; struck down, but not destroyed.
	2 Corinthians 4:8, 9

The psalmist, David, though anointed by God to be a king, was yet a desperate fugitive fleeing from King Saul's relentless pursuit and murderous intent. David composed this Psalm in his hideout in the Cave in Adullam. It was here that those who were in debt, in danger, and discontented began gathering and slowly forming an army of mighty men who, unlikely as they seemed, would all in God's time lead to the kingship (1 Sam. 22:1-2).

David, in deep dejection and desperate need, in the cave:
Declared the Lord his refuge.
Cried aloud to the Lord
Lifted his voice to the Lord for mercy
Poured out his complaint before Him
Told the Lord of his trouble
Pleaded with the Lord to rescue him from his pursuers who were too strong for him.

For it is you who know my way.

Was it in the voicing, the laying out before the Lord the details of his situation, the problems he was up against, that they shrunk down to size before the Almighty whom David came to realize "knows my way"? Was it then

David's thinking began to clear and he began to envision the way through the difficulties? Did he begin to see the men surrounding him in a new light?

Prayer:
Father, thank You. I realize as did David, it is You who know my way. So, no matter how hard pressed, crushed, perplexed, persecuted, and struck down I may be, it is through me that You choose to reveal Yourself. You will never abandon me.

_____
_____
_____
_____
_____
_____
_____
_____

Psalm 143: Outwardly Wasting Away, Inwardly Renewed

Focus Verse:	New Testament Verse:
Let the morning bring me word of your unfailing love, for I have put my trust in you.	Therefore we do not lose heart. Though outwardly we are wasting away, yet inwardly we are being renewed day by day.
Show me the way I should go, for to you I lift up my soul. (8)	2 Corinthians 4:16

This, the last of the Penitential Psalms, is a prayer of David, prayed while he was yet in his time of darkness and dismay, but focused now on seeking God's mercy for his own sinfulness. David remembers, meditates, considers, and spreads out his hands as his very soul thirsts for his God.

Notice his requests:

Hear
  Listen
    Come
      Answer (quickly)
        Do not hide
          Bring me word of your unfailing love
            Show me the way I should go
              Teach me to do your will
                Lead me on level ground
                  Bring me out of trouble
                    Silence my enemies
                      Destroy my foes

David recognized his worst foe, even when surrounded by evil men who sought to destroy him, was his own proneness to sin. It was for this that he prayed, seeking God's help, not just to know God's will, but to be taught how to do God's will. Not just to be shown God's way, but how to walk in that way.

Prayer:
Father, thank You that You are renewing me day by day.

Psalm 144: Unceasing Prayer

Focus Verse:	New Testament Verse:
blessed are the people whose God is the LORD. (15b)	With this in mind, we constantly pray for you, that our God may count you worthy of his calling and that by his power he may fulfill every good purpose of yours and every act prompted by your faith. 2 Thessalonians 1:11

This Psalm of David was composed when he had become king. Phrases from earlier Psalms of David are recognized in this "new song" to his God. It is a new song in that in this song, David as king yet recognizes his utter dependence and that of his people on the One who gives victories to kings, who trains hands for war and fingers for battle, who is their everlasting fortress, stronghold, deliverer, shield, and refuge.

If only we as individuals, as a body of believers, as a country, would live with this constant realization of our utter need for the protection and power of the risen Lord in our lives. If only we would submit to His training for the battle against sin that we all face in our lives. If only we would daily rise to sing a new song of prayer and praise, of yielding to His will so we could victoriously face each day.

For blessed are the people whose God is the Lord.

Prayer:
Father, help us to seek You and Ywill first and to pray without ceasing.

_____
_____
_____
_____
_____
_____
_____
_____

Psalm 145: Blessed is She Who Has Believed

Focus Verse:	New Testament Verse:
Your kingdom is an everlasting kingdom, and your dominion endures through all generations. The LORD is faithful to all his promises and loving toward all he has made. (13)	"Blessed is she who has believed that what the Lord has said to her will be accomplished!" Luke 1:45

Reading this psalm of praise of David, as it happens on an Easter morning, the verse that came to mind regarding the Lord's faithfulness to all His promises was a much-treasured verse recorded in Luke 1, the words of Elizabeth upon greeting Mary as both anticipated the birth of their miracle sons.

Blessed is she who has believed that what the Lord has said to her will be accomplished. (Luke 1:45)

Fast forward to the first Easter morning. Mary Magdalene stood outside Christ's empty tomb weeping, waiting for what she did not know. But waiting and watching and weeping. Tears clouding her vision, she did not recognize the man standing *outside* the tomb until He spoke her name: *"Mary."*
"Rabboni."
She alone was there to greet the risen Lord.
Do I, like Mary, push forward, purely out of my profound love for Him and my deep trust in Him:
- even if I do not understand completely (neither did Mary)?

- even if I am not sure what to do (but she did what she could by preparing and taking the spices, and waiting, watching, weeping)?
- even if there seems no way to overcome the obstacles (the heavy stone blocking the tomb entrance)?

For, what He has said to her will, against all odds, in spite of the visible circumstances, be accomplished.

Another important theme of this Psalm is one generation commending the Lord's work to another: His mighty acts, His glorious splendor and majesty, His power and awesome works, His great deeds, abundant goodness and righteousness, His graciousness, compassion, and mercy to all of His creation.

Prayer:

Father, I have a whole quiver full of nieces and nephews. I have a church full of children and infants, with more on the way. What can I do? Help me, Father, find as many opportunities as possible to:

❖ Commend Your works
❖ Tell of Your mighty acts
❖ Speak of the glorious splendor of Your majesty
❖ Meditate on Your wonderful works
❖ Tell of the power of Your awesome works
❖ Proclaim Your great deeds
❖ Celebrate Your abundant goodness
❖ Joyfully sing of Your righteousness

One generation to another.

Psalm 146: Our Personal Praise

Focus Verse:	New Testament Verse:
Blessed is he whose help is in the God of Jacob, whose hope is in the LORD his God, (5)	"The Lord is my helper." Hebrews 13:6

Our journey through the Psalms ends with five Psalms of pure praise. This the first, the personal praise song of David: *Praise the Lord, O my soul...*

This is a soul who has found his Jehovah God to be all-sufficient, who has maintained a right view of God and thus lives a life of perpetual praise.

God is:
- His helper
- His hope
- The maker of heaven and Earth
- Worker of justice
- Provider
- Deliverer
- Restorer of sight
- The Lifter of those who are bowed down
- Righteous
- Vigilant
- The Sustainer
- Against the crooked

The Lord reigns forever, for all generations.
How fitting the great hymn of faith as our prayer...

Prayer:
Be Thou my vision, O Lord of my life
Naught be all else to me save that Thou art

Thou my best thought by day or by night,
Waking or sleeping, Thy presence my light.
(Mary Elizabeth Byrne, 1905)

_____

_____

_____

_____

_____

_____

_____

_____

Psalm 147: Joining Others In Praise

Focus Verse:	New Testament Verse:
Great is our Lord and mighty in power; his understanding has no limit. (5)	Therefore, since we have a great high priest who has gone through the heavens, Jesus the Son of God, let us hold firmly to the faith we profess. For we do not have a high priest who is unable to sympathize with our weaknesses, but we have one who has been tempted in every way, just as we are-yet was without sin. Let us then approach the throne of grace with confidence, so that we may receive mercy and find grace to help us in our time of need. Hebrews 4:14-16

Here, a Psalm of praise to be sung by the inhabitants of Jerusalem, by the returning exiles, by the house of Jacob, the nation to whom God chose to reveal His Word.
Praise the Lord.
It is good, pleasant, and fitting to praise the Lord:
- ❖ He builds up Jerusalem
- ❖ He gathers the exiles of Israel
- ❖ He heals the brokenhearted
- ❖ He binds up their wounds
- ❖ He is mighty in power
- ❖ His understanding has no limit
- ❖ He sustains the humble but casts the wicked to the ground
- ❖ He not only created the stars, He counted and named each one.

This mighty creator and sustainer God delights in those who fear Him, who put their hope in His unfailing love.

Prayer:
Thank You, Father, that I am invited in to the very throne room of heaven because of what Jesus did for me. Thank You for His understanding of my struggles, His compassion, and His sufficient grace.

Psalm 148: All Heaven and Earth Praise

Focus Verse:	New Testament Verse:
Let them praise the name of the LORD, for his name alone is exalted; his splendor is above the earth and the heavens. (13)	For since the creation of the world God's invisible qualities-his eternal power and divine nature-have been clearly seen, being understood from what has been made, so that men are without excuse.
	Romans 1:20

This hymn of praise is to be sung by all of heaven and Earth. Praising Him from the heights of heaven:
- His angels
- His heavenly hosts
- The sun, moon, and stars
- The highest heaven
- The waters above the skies

For He commanded and they were created, setting them in place for ever and ever.

Praising Him from the earth:
- The great sea creatures and all ocean depths
- Lightning, hail, snow, clouds, stormy winds
- Mountains and all hills, fruit trees, and cedars
- Wild animals, all cattle, small creatures, and flying birds
- Kings of the earth and of all nations, young and old men, and maidens and children

For His name alone is exalted. He has raised up for His people a horn (a King), a Savior-for the people close to His heart (v. 14).

                    His name is JESUS.

Prayer:
Thank You for revealing Jesus to us.

Psalm 149: Praising with a New Song

Focus Verse:	New Testament Verse:
Praise the LORD. Sing to the LORD a new song, his praise in the assembly of the saints. (1)	"It is not for you to know the times or dates the Father has set by his own authority." Acts 1:7

In this penultimate Psalm, the call is for a song of praise by the assembly of the saints, specifically Israel, the people of Zion, God's chosen ones. Not just singing, but dancing, accompanied by instruments.

For the Lord takes delight in His people. He crowns the humble with salvation. God will ultimately work justice on this earth and righteousness triumphs over evil.

We do not know the day or the hour, but we can rejoice and praise the Lord that evil will one day be destroyed.

Prayer:

Until that day, Father, I live in the knowledge that You delight in me. Lead us to delight in You, to praise You with unbridled joy, for Your gift of salvation and to know with certainty and contentment that You will ultimately triumph over all sin, evil, and death. I need not know the day or the hour, only trust in You.

Psalm 150: Praise the Lord in Everything!

Focus Verse:	New Testament Verse:
Let everything that has breath praise the LORD. Praise the LORD. (6)	Is any one of you in trouble? He should pray. Is anyone happy? Let him sing songs of praise.
	James 5:13

This is a doxology, thus the fitting conclusion of this last Psalm of this fifth of the five Books of Psalms.

Praise the Lord, for He is:

Mighty
    Exalted
        Powerful
            Great
                He acts

All who have breath, praise the Lord with:

Harp
    Lyre
        Tambourine
            Dancing
                Strings
                    Flute
                        Cymbals

This Psalm invites unbridled joy, jubilant celebration, extravagant expression, as all God's creatures praise Him for who He is and what He has done on our behalf.

        Praise the Lord!

I love the rendering of this Psalm by Linda Sattgast in her delightful, *Bedtime Psalms for Little Ones (used with permission of the author):*

Praise the Lord
BOOM ba-ba BOOM
Bangs the big brass drum.
PLAASHH... PLAASHH
Sound the cymbals
TAH ra-ta TAH
All the trumpets shout.
TOO la-la TOO
Cries the flute.
TAP TAP TAP
Go the dancing feet.
All of the children play and sing.
Everyone is saying the very same thing
PRAISE THE LORD
In everything!
(Sattgast, 1994)

Prayer:
Father, God, I praise You. In everything!

Conclusion

Leaving Green Pastures and Quiet Waters

Concluding thoughts on making the transition from this prolonged time of rest in the green pastures, and restoration and healing beside the quiet waters to embark once again under the guidance of the Great Shepherd on the paths of righteousness.

I will fear no evil, Psalm 23:4	I press on toward the goal to win the prize for which God has called me heavenward in Christ Jesus. Philippians 3:14

Approaching the end of the Psalms, around Psalm 145 or so, I began digging in my heels and dragging my feet, sometimes spending an extra day or two on each remaining precious Psalm. I was reluctant to leave the green pastures, I wanted to linger a bit longer beside the quiet waters, letting the healing words deeply restore my soul. Soon, though, I knew, it would be time for the

Good Shepherd to urge me onward into the paths of righteousness where I will learn daily, minute-by-minute obedience. Perhaps too the pathway will lead through the Valley of the Shadow of Death, I considered with a twinge of anxiety, but then, *I will fear no evil.*

This I have learned with unflinching certainty in my months in the Psalms: *for You are with me.*

Yes, it is time for me to press on. *To press on toward the goal to win the prize for which God has called me heavenward in Christ Jesus (Phil. 3:14).*

It is important to recognize these seasons of life and to be open and sensitive to the Shepherd's guidance in our lives. Being willing to lie down and rest when needed, to draw away from the busyness of work and service to spend time beside the quiet waters, to sit at His footstool, gaze into His face, and learn of His ways.

I began to realize during this time the Good Shepherd had also been fitting my feet with readiness-the very feet I was now dragging and digging in. He has been making my feet like the feet of a deer, enabling me to stand on the heights (Ps. 18:33), preparing me to journey ever higher.

Father, You have prepared me for my first steps back on the paths of righteousness. Orient me heavenward. I want to press on toward the goal to which You have called me. Onward and upward!

The End.

Record your own pleading and praising.
Write out your treasured verses.
Share with someone who needs to be encouraged today.

_____
_____
_____
_____
_____
_____
_____
_____
_____
_____

References

Boom, C. t. (1971). *The Hiding Place* . Grand Rapids, MI: Chosen Books .

Bunyan, J. (1678). *Pilgrim's Progress.*

Edwards, J. (n.d.). *Goodreads*. Retrieved from The Works of Jonathan Edwards, Vol. 17: Sermons and Discourses, 1730-1733

Godden, R. (1964). *In This House of Breede.* New York City : Open Road Integrated Media .

Lewis, C. S. (1953). *The Chronicles of Narnia: The Silver Chair.* New York: Harper Collins.

Longfellow, H. W. (1865). *I Heard the Bells on Christmas Day.* Ticknor and Fields in Our Young Folks.

Morgan, G. C. (1994). *Life Applications From Every Chapter of the Bible.* Grand Rapids: Fleming H. Revell.

Nee, W. (n.d.). *SermonIndex.net*. Retrieved from Sermon Index: http://www.sermonindex.net/modules/articles/index.php?view=article&aid=1865

Sattgast, L. J. (1994). *Bedtime Psalms for Little Ones.* Sisters, OR: Gold'n Honey a Division of Questar Publishers, Inc.

Spurgeon, C. (1971). *Twelve Sermons on Prayer.* Ada, Michigan: Baker Books. Retrieved from https://www.goodreads.com/quotes/333739-prayer-is-the-slender-nerve-that-moves-the-muscle-of